CW01671779

VOYAGES

A Reading Writers' Anthology

First published in Great Britain in 2014 by St. Marks Publishing
21 St Marks Road, Henley-on-Thames, Oxon, RG9 1LP

10 9 8 7 6 5 4 3 2 1

ISBN 978-0-9572636-1-1

Typeset in Garamond by Andy Bennett

FSC sustainable

Printed and bound in Great Britain by KnowledgePoint Limited, Wokingham, Berkshire.

FSC

Also available as an eBook

readingwriters.wordpress.com

Contents

Acknowledgements

As editor of the 2014 Reading Writers' anthology it has been my privilege to bring together an amazing range of stories and poems by a wonderful group of writers.

I'd like to thank everyone who seized the idea of an anthology with gusto and contributed their time and talents to it. I would particularly like to thank the Mighty Subcommittee – Claire Dyer, Judy Hodgetts and Richard Chalmers – for shielding me from pitfalls, and the Proofreading Army – Juliet England, Hanne Larsson, Steve Partridge, John Shepherd, Rose Renshaw and Julia Bohanna – for reading things over and over again. Many thanks also to Josh Williams for being my right-hand man in countless ways, Alana James for sharing her invaluable experience as editor of the 2011 Reading Writers' anthology, and Andy Bennett for typesetting the collection with such care, as well as providing beautiful ideas for the cover design. Charles Whittaker has my eternal gratitude for organising printing and providing insight into the production process and material assistance. Our cover would be nothing without artistic talents of India Bohanna and the design expertise of Tracey R. Jones. I'd also like to thank Kit Berry for writing us a lovely foreword, Chapter One bookshop in Woodley for hosting a wonderful launch party, KnowledgePoint for printing the book and Julie Cohen for answering Holmesian queries.

M. K. Lloyd
Editor

ABC to Read

Assisting Berkshire Children to Read

ABC to Read is a local charity in Reading. We recruit, train and support community volunteers to provide one-to-one mentoring of primary school children who are struggling to read. We work to advance the education and self-confidence of primary school children in Berkshire by helping them to overcome reading difficulties, making reading fun and giving them a skill for life while promoting their general well-being. We're always looking for volunteers. Find out more at *www.abctoread.org.uk*.

Foreword

I am delighted to introduce this collection of stories and poems created by Reading Writers. I visited them one dark winter's night to talk about my own writing, and was charmed by their warmth and enthusiasm. *Voyages* reflects the group's diversity and eclecticism, and is a wonderful showcase for their collective talent.

A voyage is travel or a journey, sometimes ending up at the very point of departure. In a way, a story – short or long, poetry or prose – is the same. It starts and ends, and ideally, the bit in the middle is interesting and enlightening. So it is with this entertaining anthology.

Life itself is a voyage, of course. I first visited Reading in the early 1960s with my mother, to buy school uniform at Heelas. The long list included obsolete items such as 'grey knickers, five pairs' and 'grey felt hat with headband'. A lifetime and much travel later, I now live in Reading. I was firmly rooted in beautiful Dorset, where all my books are set and where my soul lies. But not my heart, it seems. That was won by a Reading man who took me on the greatest voyage of all. So here I am today, another local author, and honoured to introduce *Voyages.*

Enjoy the stories and poetry in this volume. Some pieces will resonate more than others because we read through our personal lens, and by the end, you may feel as I did – refreshed, stimulated and with a new awareness. What more could anyone ask of a voyage?

Kit Berry, author of The Stonewylde Series
Reading, May 2014, www.kitberry.com

DEPARTURE

The Calgary Stampede

Steve Partridge

My father never read proper books. He read gunfighter fiction. Zane Grey and J. T. Edson. At the dinner table he did very poor cowboy impersonations to impress his five year old son: 'Hey bud, pass me the pepper.' I passed him the yellow plastic pepper pot; he blanketed his food with white pepper, and then burst into a sneezing fit. When he had recovered, he told me stories about the Wild West, the Great Depression and the Calgary Stampede.

In 1931, aged 21, and 17 years before I was born, my father emigrated to Calgary, Alberta, with my grandmother. They arrived in March, and were taken in by my aunt and her Canadian husband. After the premature death of my grandfather in 1926, my grandmother wanted to be close to her daughter and her grandchildren. My father, jobless at the time, told me stories of people who queued at Salvation Army soup kitchens twice a day for food, of hobos, who, without the price of a bed for the night, froze to death in shop doorways. And of 200 men who scrambled to get to the front of a factory gate to fight over three job vacancies. In June, his luck changed when he found a job as a roustabout with the Calgary Stampede, maintaining fences, mucking out animals, selling popcorn.

My wife and I touched down in Calgary on the 4th July 2003, 72 years after my father's arrival. The airport concourse was decked out with wagon wheels, bales of straw, and Wanted posters. As we left immigration our hands were rubber stamp branded with the legend 'Calgary Stampede'.

Near the exit a country band was playing *Hey Mammas Don't Let Your Children Grow Up To Be Cowboys*. Cowboys shook our hands, welcomed us to Stampede Week, then pointed us in the direction of taxis and hotel courtesy buses.

The next day we entered The Stampede for the bull riding. The programme told us bull riding is the epitome of rodeo riding. The bull rider has to stay on the bull for at least eight seconds before his time is officially recorded. One hand is secured to the animal by a rope, the other one is free, used for balance only. As the event was about to start, I had an urge to return to the stadium concourse to see if my father was working on the popcorn stand. But I remained seated.

The voice of rodeo announcer Dave Poulsen painted the picture: 'From Glendive, Montana, on Outlaw, Cody Jesse! I wanna tell you, folks, Outlaw is seventeen hundred pounds of pure bovine locomotion. He's one rank hombre. Good luck, Cody! You'll need it! Open the chute!'

Outlaw charged into the arena, Cody Jesse bounced about on his back like an electrocuted rag doll. The bull's back legs kicked out, his front legs were off the ground. He thrashed, twisted and turned. Rider and bull span in a swirling vortex of dust. After 9.6 seconds, Jesse was tossed into the air and crashed to the ground.

'Hey, folks, what a ride by Cody Jesse. He's one tough cowboy! That showground floor is a hard as a woodpecker's lips.' We joined in with the crowd and roared our appreciation.

Early evening brought us the chuck wagon races, a throwback to chariot racing in a Roman hippodrome. Chuck wagon racing has four rigs in each heat, and there are nine heats. The wagon is pulled by four horses, and has a driver and four outriders. The course is a figure of eight, five-eighths of a mile long.

'In heat nine, we have, from Grande Prairie, Alberta, ten times Calgary Stampede champion, Kelly Sutherland!' The flag went down, Sutherland was straight out in front, around the first barrel that marked out the course, closely followed by Herman Flad, of Bodo, Alberta. As the rigs galloped away, Flad was challenging Sutherland, we could hear the crack of his whip as he nearly caught the leader at the second barrel. The two other rigs trailed behind, swallowing the front men's dust. Sutherland and Flad rounded the last barrel and raced to the finish. Another crack of Flad's whip, but Sutherland inched his rig over the line, just qualified for the final. Eat your heart out, Ben Hur!

We ended our day with a visit to the revolving top of the Calgary Tower. As we rotated, taking in the panorama, a news crew assembled by the lift doors. The director shouted, 'Get ready!'

Out of the lift came a cowboy on a horse. The crazy-eyed animal walked forward, raised its front legs for the camera. As I looked at the cowboy, his face morphed into my father's face. For a moment I thought ... the image melted away. The crew got their footage, we went around one more time, then headed back to our hotel.

Room service delivered our dinner: rib eye steaks with fries, side salad, French mustard, condiments. I turned on the news to see if it really was my old man on the back of the horse at the top of the tower. As they showed the shot of the lift door opening, I heard a voice next to me say, 'Hey bud, pass me the pepper.' Instinctively, I picked up the pepper pot; turned to my right to acknowledge my father's voice. But there was nobody there. Penny looked at me as though I was crazy.

Then back again to the TV to check the screen. The shot of the cowboy leaving the lift on his horse had faded. The camera panned over the Calgary skyline, over downtown office blocks, the hockey stadium, The Stampede and fairground. Inside my head, I smelled burgers and bratwurst, tasted the burn of mustard and onions on my tongue, heard the slap of a stick on a puck, saw the incandescent lights of the rides flashing in the night sky. The voice next to me had gone; it had soared away, like an eagle on a thermal, back home to the rodeo, to live alongside the cowboys' cries, the roar of the crowd, the crescendo of wagon wheels, and horses' hooves. And that is where it belonged, forever, with the Calgary Stampede.

Flying to Miami

Robert Billing

Lumbering over lumpy, bumpy tarmac
Boeing, whale-ungainly, slipping free from Earth,
Chasing Autumn's watery, waning sun,
Mid-morning, coffee-scented, punctuated by airport lights.

Sun, marking out our hours with its path,
Is stilled within the heavens by our pace,
We fly, no smoking and the seat belt sign,
Ungainly fowl, fouled by baggage and our duty-frees.

Hours pass, picked out by meals and drinks,
Time into flight, the ever present now,
No longer GMT as Greenwich falls astern,
We age no more as sun stands still in changing sky.

Without eleven what now becomes elevenses?
A little touch, the sun swings to the right,
Our captain turns us south, his voice crisp on the intercom,
Warm and ageless in easy reassurance.

We wind the seasons back as we run south,
The snow lies crisp on winter ground, then gold and green,
Forest, rivers, cities standing proud beneath us,
As we trade space for time and summer comes again.

Yet deeper still, time's sweet influence,
Reaches us within our grey light-alloy bird,
We've left our lives behind in time from time,
Wheels touch, we remember,

And once again are young.

The Good Earth

Eileen Dickson

I sit back on my heels and look with satisfaction at the row of young lettuce plants now settled into the thin earth in their own little puddles of water. Prakash will shake his head at yet another instance of my English foolishness.

I love this time of the morning. The sun has not yet fully risen, the air is cool, and there is still a faint dampness on the earth. We're lucky here on the hillside where I can collect firewood for the stove; they are *selling* it on Niwas Street! There is a respectful cough behind me.

'Carrots, Madam,' Prakash reproves sadly. 'Or beetroots. Beetroots is good for here.'

We may be considered *poor whites,* but to Prakash, I am always 'Madam.'

'Thank you, Prakash,' I reply, 'but Sir does not like carrots and beetroots remind me of school dinners.'

*

I'd met Roland Firth at the local university where I was hungrily catching up on lost education. Roland taught economics and flirted with his students. Impressed by his academic aura and undoubted charm, I was flattered when he chose me. The university was less impressed by previous near-run incidents with young female students, and threw him out. He'd chosen Udaipur for our 'escape' because of its *cultural heritage,* and I believed him, much as I believed he had money and would divorce his wife. And here I am, on a hillside in Udaipur with dwindling savings, and an elderly, bad-tempered man to whom I'm not married.

'Good morning, Mrs Firth, I hope I find you well?'

God, was it that time already? Mrs Chatergee is standing by the garden gate, an amazing picture in white high-heeled shoes, matching handbag and shiny navy blue suit.

'Am I a little early for you? I will tell my driver to wait while you get ready perhaps?'

Criticism of my crumpled trousers and muddy hands hangs unspoken in the morning air.

'Not at all, Mrs Chatergee. It won't take a moment for me to change, but real linen always creases, don't you find?'

We start on our mutually enjoyable exchange of put-downs, officially known as 'English lessons'. Mrs Chatergee's husband owned the Udaipur Uretha Factory which made them wealthy. It had not, in his wife's opinion, given her the social standing to which she felt entitled. We'd met at a grim British Council function where she'd suggested we could be *mutually beneficial:* in exchange for lessons on English culture, she would reciprocate with Indian. 'Although of course, Mrs Firth, I consider myself *Rajashthani* rather than just Indian. Descended from the Moguls, you know.'

I'd courageously suggested to her that *money* would be far more acceptable.

'Of course, Mrs Firth, I understand, though I am a little surprised. I had thought Dr Firth to be a University Man.'

Dr Firth? Where had that sprung from?

'Indeed so, Mrs Chatergee, but he has sacrificed his academic career in order to concentrate on his book, *Myths of Civilization.*'

'Oh certainly, it must be a privilege looking after a great literary man.'

Well perhaps it was, *if* I was, I thought, recalling empty whisky bottles and dirty socks strewn round our bedroom.

'You will of course,' she went on, 'have dined at our beautiful Lake Palace Hotel?'

We'd only been to their *'Eat as Much as You Like for 150 Rupees'* buffet after we'd first arrived, and it was certainly a most beautiful palace, set on an island on Lake Pichola. But because of our lack of money, any further meals out had been at Kwality Restaurant on Station Road. Cheaper still was Ravi's, where he always seated us in the window to encourage the tourists.

I'd replied instead: 'We enjoyed our dinner there, but Dr Firth finds that it aids his digestion to eat more simply. Compared to that, surroundings are unimportant.'

'Oh I do understand, but is it not "compared *with*"? Please forgive if this is not so.'

I seated her firmly on the veranda, blessing the rambling bougainvillea and hibiscus, which not only gave it shade, but also held the rotting timbers together. The punkah fan had broken and the house was already hot, but I could make tea quickly so that we could drink it outside. Roland hopefully would not appear until after lunch, but you never knew. It depended largely on the quantity of Black Monk he'd drunk the previous evening. I nagged him about drinking local whisky with his high blood pressure, but he told me it was now his one true pleasure. As I, obviously, was not. I made the tea, and covering the tin tray with an embroidered linen cloth, took it out to the veranda. I wanted to get back to Mrs Chatergee before she could go on the prowl, and discover the true frugality of our existence. But before we'd agreed on the exact protocol of calling cards, Roland appeared. He was unshaven and unsteady on his feet. His dressing gown flapped open at the front. His unsteady hand held a glass from which slopped some dark liquid. And he was very, very angry.

'Bloody hell, woman, what you doing with visitors – can't you see I'm workin'?'

No, in very truth, I could not see that. The fact that *I* was, and bringing in some small income, was lost on him. He lurched a little and fixed Mrs Chatergee with a stare.

'You come for the cleaning job? No banging the pots in the kitchen eh, there's a good girl. Need it quiet for my writing.'

Mrs Chatergee spilt some tea down the impeccable navy suit and stood up.

'Please call my chauffeur,' she managed. 'We are all done here.'

Roland blundered away, and later I heard a crash at the back of the house. I was so angry I did not go to investigate.

*

The turnout at the tiny British cemetery was surprisingly good, especially since Roland had offended most of our few acquaintances.

Almighty God, we commend the soul of our brother Roland

The sun now shone directly overhead, bouncing off the cheap brass coffin handles. I felt sorry for the grave-digger who'd had to hack away at the baked earth.

Earth to earth, ashes to ashes, dust to dust

I knew clearly then what I wanted to do. I wanted to go *round* the Earth, not *into* it. I reached down to the bag by my side, and drew out the manuscript of *Myths of Civilisation.* The mourners were patient, as page by page, I floated them down onto the coffin. A slight breeze came from nowhere, and they eddied and fluttered into the grave.

Later, Prakash came silently up to stand beside me. Together we looked down at the little lettuces, now turning yellow – either through too much watering or too much sun – or perhaps too much love? No, there could never be too much love.

'I think, Madam, that they are now died. They not meant for here.'

And neither was I.

We smiled at each other and solemnly shook hands.

'Beetroots will be better,' he said.

Hope

Tahereh Zoghi

Oh Hope, see how you are taking me over:
bit by bit pushing back the bleak past
as you revealed the alluring vista
of a town of innate beauty,
famed for literature and poetry.

Oh my Hope, see what you've done:
ever since that tantalizing taste,
the pull of darkness is fading away,
now that you've shown me the sight,
now that I've witnessed its light.

In the sleep of aeons life had turned,
though sleep can be full of soft dreams.
Means for travelling were not fast.
But now waking brings me face to face
with things erstwhile covered in darkness.

Look, how hard I am now trying
not to be blinded in the full glare,
or to lose my fragile bearing
in the face of such a strong light –
to keep the balance of my frail heart.

And now I'm frightened of waking
since I see in you signs of weakness.
Oh my Hope, don't ever leave me,
now that you have shown me the sight,
now that I have witnessed its light.

Not Winners

Andy Bennett

I do wonder why I enter writing competitions. The outcome is always the same, and this was no different. Yet again, I was a los– No, I can't bring myself to say it, we are all winners, just that some are winners without prizes, or anyone left to be a runner up. Still, I'm trying hard to convince myself. Like a prize fighter, if I tell myself enough, it will be true. Yes, I'm on the up and already winning in some ways. Just look at that array of trophies.

Well, not trophies, not even a cabinet in planning. Really the closest so far are some plastic flowers and a set of horrible crockery, still boxed and consigned to the back of a cupboard, acting as a symbol of a wedding day and the lack of ability in some guests to recognise brown as a bad colour for plates. They are not even mine. I didn't win them in the subsequently failed marriage to which they truly belong. I got them as a gift since the proper recipient no longer needed them clogging up his cupboard.

I was his and his partner's lodger at the time, and one day I got a call. It was bad news and we needed to meet. So, we did later that day after work.

'Andy,' he'd said, 'it's over.' I have to say, I wondered what I'd done, and why a phone call wasn't good enough. I was worried I might not be allowed to return that night.

I searched my mind looking for things. I couldn't remember breaking the bathroom, or being overly offensive. If anything the conversation might have been too mundane – which I hope wasn't criminal in itself. I definitely was using their shampoo without asking, but surely that wasn't enough reason for eviction.

No, that wasn't it. 'She's leaving me. She's been seeing another man and is leaving to be with him.'

I was shocked; I wasn't prepared for someone else going. And how are you supposed to react on hearing of a friend's marriage break-up anyway:

1. Provide forward-looking support: 'It's okay, mate,' and give him a manly back slap hug, 'there are plenty more fish in the sea.'
2. Show compassion, by touching him firmly on the shoulder and saying, 'There there, mate. What a cow.'
3. Or maybe even just think of myself and see what my outlook was: 'Okay, I can still stay can't I?'

'Oh…' I replied succinctly, not often being blessed with much emotional foresight. The rest of the conversation I don't remember, but the whole situation led to some awkwardness as she didn't leave immediately. I couldn't help but feel slightly like a third spoke in this relationship, albeit just a bit part spoke, and that, in a small way, she was leaving me too.

Finally it became just the two of us. Two men together – grrr! – until he did meet his next fish and move on, which meant my moving on too. This was the true origin of the crockery, as at that time I had few domestic possessions.

'Here, we never opened it; you might as well have them for your flat? They're…' he looked at the box and then back at me, 'nice.'

'Okay…' I looked down too and pulled a similar face – there was a good reason they were still boxed. 'Thanks.' Still I took them, but filed them immediately at the back of the cupboard where they've been since.

So, maybe the plates are no symbol of success, but at least I can feel somewhat superior to them, kept in that cupboard with the tiered cake tray, knobbly glass punch bowl, and vase with a pig design. At least I see daylight, so yes, a win in the 'not being stuck in a cupboard' stakes – I hold my hand shaped like an 'L' to my forehead to you plates. Well, I would if I could be bothered to wade through the other things in the cupboard.

Still, the plates and I can share in one thing: we likely both had the same inability to come up with good ideas following the announcement of the writing group's competition's theme. It is with some dread that I await it since I know it will be hard work to come up with anything. I do have some diligence in wanting to enter however, so I felt it mandatory to come up with something no matter how tortured the process.

So, along came the day of the announcement, dispatched via an email from the secretary. It declared the theme as … 'Earth', backed with a big picture of a planet as a subtle subliminal reminder of one of the meanings. I despaired, as all I could think of were big clods of mud, and had to wonder how possibly I could build that into something deep and meaningful? I could almost guarantee too that there would be some entries with themes woven like delicate lace tapestries of emotion and subtlety just waiting to caress the reader's eyes on the page. That was, unless I was very lucky and a large part of the group got conveniently called away on business at the same time.

No, mud wasn't going to cut it; I needed something proper, deep and subtle. Well, as it happened, I found myself in a hotel in Southend-on-Sea over that Easter, as I'm sure many a Booker Prize winner has before me, and it was there I found the spark of genius.

Southend is the home of a thriving seaside tourist industry; it has the longest leisure pier in the UK, and its fair share of culture and history too. That hadn't stopped the torrential rain on my arrival however, nor the effect on my demeanour as I squelched through the town centre, towards my hotel and a diminishing expectation of an enjoyable break. Behind the wall of water, my hotel lurked in a spot on the cliff top, overlooking the pleasure beach and the famously long pier.

I checked in and went to my room to change my wet things. I looked out of the window at the continuing rainfall and hoped the next day might be better. I wasn't expecting much of a view as late-availability-super-saver rates don't often come with expansive panoramas – that is assuming there is a window at all. The first glance revealed the all too predictable car park, but there was something else that clicked deep in my psyche. There, like a shining beacon of literary inspiration on the right of the car park, was a graveyard!

Wow, I thought, it doesn't get deeper than that, buried people and stuff, and not only that; they're all wrapped in mud! Well, I can't claim the story just flowed; my aim to have the piece finished by my return from Southend failed miserably. Many more days of procrastination and false starts followed, but eventually the piece was completed, a story of crime, passion, emotion, double-crossing, but mostly about exhuming and reburying a cat.

So, off it went to the judges. Part of me hoped secretly that they would identify extreme genius and layers of subtle meaning, but I did also know half the group hadn't been taken away on business and as such my chances of success might have been dwindling even before I pressed send.

The piece became forgotten, behind the toils of everyday life, until eventually the night of the results. Hay fever was in my nostrils and my mood was distinctly not favourable. I sat by an open window, my nose streaming and eyes tired and intolerant.

People read one by one. The group applauded each in celebration, followed immediately by a review from the judges to remind the author that they shouldn't be complacent and that actually the plot might be thin, and the characters flat. I wasn't paying the best attention and my head was spinning a little. Maybe it was creating a delusion, but still I was hopeful. I would be invited to read and then … and then, declaration of my having supplied a beautiful tale of family woes and an evolving relationship between father and son, albeit expressed through the medium of a dead cat.

My time hadn't come by the time of the top three, nor the top two, or even by the announcement of the winner. I held my breath, and listened intently as the judges began to describe their reasons for selecting first place, keeping us teased throughout as to who it was.

The piece sounded magnificent as they spoke about its emotional impact, the characters and the setting. There were a couple of doubts forming in my mind at this point, however. The words 'cat' and 'graveyard' hadn't appeared in their description much, or at all actually, and really the characters weren't sounding right, but may be they were focusing on some hidden meaning that I hadn't noticed during writing.

The judge paused, adding further to the tension. 'Come on … get on with it… Graveyard! Cat!' I screamed in my mind, subliminally willing them to say my name … but no, there had been too many entries to read them all. I was joint prize-less fourth again, shared with everyone else who was also in the winning-but-without-prize category.

I went home disappointed, walked into the kitchen and waved another 'L' in the direction of the cupboard. That crockery still wasn't coming out. Then I thought … the plates are brown … the colour of earth. So, even they are better fitted to the theme than me. I sank deeper into despair, second even to a plate. That is a new low!

Goldfish

Robert Billing

The goldfish was the first to die. A pity really, as he'd been a mascot for our colony. He'd swum around in a tank that one of the technicians had carved from the remains of a plastic reagent bottle and placed on a shelf immediately inside the airlock. All the goldfish did was blow bubbles at everyone who went in or out – but he was a gently reassuring presence, a reminder of Old Earth.

Goldfish take quite easily to suspended animation. Their body chemistry allows them to freeze and thaw without too much damage. Which is why the old-style colony ships carried a shoal of the things, frozen as little fishypops, in the liquid nitrogen tanks. And the computers used them as indicators. The program would thaw out a goldfish and observe its behaviour, then use this data to recalibrate the revival process before thawing out the colonists.

Our first goldfish – we called him Thor for obvious reasons – had survived the process and become a pet. We'd promised him a pond of his own, and a lady goldfish, just as soon as the terraforming advanced far enough to let him breathe. There was a natural pond only a hundred yards from where we'd landed and every week we analysed the water. It had started off with enough dissolved ammonia to work as a highly effective bleach. But as the terraforming reactions kicked in hard the atmospheric ammonia was fixed into the soil and the reducing gases, mainly hydrogen and methane, went down fast. There was more and more carbon dioxide, day by day, until the morning when the digital Orsat announced the first oxygen.

Then the race was on. When would the dissolved oxygen in the pond get up to the point that Thor could be released?

He didn't make it. As the atmosphere went through the high carbon dioxide phase, before the carbon got trapped in biomass, we had a greenhouse period. The temperature went way up and everyone on the ship started discarding clothing. Thor went up to one end of his tank and sulked for three days before we realised that goldfish don't handle hot water very well. By the time we'd got some ice in his tank he was badly stressed, and he died a week later. Of course we thawed another goldfish – we called this one Frosty – but he wasn't the same.

We gave Thor a proper burial. We got the core drill and went down to a decent depth, then dropped him in and backfilled.

And that's why the grave of the first colonist to die on Homeworld is six feet deep, but only four inches across.

Winged Coffin

Julie Roberts

A wooden coffin, six feet long, twelve inches wide and fifteen inches deep, was strapped onto the roof rack of a car that sped southwards through the Hampshire countryside. At the Portsmouth ferry, no one questioned what was in the coffin. The stevedore signalled the car into its parking place and moved on. They didn't ask if it could be granny getting a free ride.

The French Customs men smiled, waved the car on; they found nothing unusual about seeing a coffin on a car. It could have a stash of diamonds inside – but what did they care? It would mean lots of form filling and sign language – easier to let it pass. Weaving through the busy town streets, then between fields of wheat and maize, the car and its coffin diminished into a dot along the avenue of trees.

The Belgians were as nonchalant as the Frenchmen. A nod, a glance at the gold crested passports, and then on towards the town of Liege and the *ladies of the night.* What if there had been bags of cocaine winging by?

A whizz through Luxembourg and then…

Oh, oh! The German border – now there would be an interrogation. Up went the hand – stop. Another cursory look at Her Majesty's Coat of Arms, a curt nod and off went the car and coffin into cuckoo clock land. It motored through the Moselle vine fields, alongside the Rhine and over the hills that grew into mountains.

The Swiss border had a road barrier and the customs men spoke English. Now the coffin would be opened. What was that? They only wanted to know if the car had a motorway licence. Of course it did! Find it someone and stick it on the windscreen.

The barrier was lifted and the car, with brass handles knocking against the coffin ends, passed through. They didn't care if the missing Great Train Robbery loot was inside; more pennies for the coded accounts. In the land of mountains, valleys and lakes the journey ended. On a plateau above a village, in a pasture of wild flowers, lay the coffin. The lid was lifted. Was a ritual burial about to take place?

The mystery is finally revealed – hubby's model glider and the kids' kites!

Swimming Lessons

Claire Dyer

At first Saturday mornings
at St Joseph's, too early,
water that made you blue-cold.

Neither of you wearing
water wings; my heart
round in my mouth for the hour,

the texture and weight of stone.
Then community centre pools,
a Quaker school on Thursdays at five,

sometimes cottages by the sea.
I can't recall when I first let go.
Now you slice the waves

the sun bright on your backs
and down in Kalkan Old Town
the harbour sings with the call to prayer.

ADVERSITY AND ADVENTURE

Sherlock Holmes and The Giant Rat of Sumatra

R.M.A. Renshaw

This is written out of affection for Conan Doyle's creations. Holmes purists – forgive!

For many a long year, I, Dr John Watson, humble chronicler of the intellectual brilliance of my great friend, Sherlock Holmes, in solving all manner of mysteries, considered the shocking case of The Giant Rat of Sumatra to be a tale for which the world was not yet ready. I still harbour many reservations and misgivings about committing the narrative to paper, for it is one so heinous, so ghastly and so terrible that I wonder if it would be better falling back into the shadows than being brought into the light. However, in no other instance has Holmes' insight been so acute, so it would be a disservice to my friend if I did not relate to others how much I am in his debt – for, truly, he saved us both, by a whisker, from a most awful fate. This, then, is the tale.

It was on an ordinary enough October morning that it all began. The air was crisp, and, armed with the Saturday morning edition of my favoured newspaper, I called in at 221B Baker Street to see my dear friend Holmes. It was a well-worn jest between us that I would try to surprise him with snippets quoted from the pages, and he would then casually give me an insider's view.

'Hallo there, Holmes,' I called as I was shown into his study by the excellent Mrs Hudson.

'My dear Watson,' he replied. 'What news have you to share with me today? I can see at once that Mrs Watson is well and at home pressing wildflowers.'

'Great heavens!' I exclaimed. 'How can you possibly know that? Indeed, she was taking out her press as I left.'

'It's clear enough if you would only apply my methods,' rejoined Holmes calmly. 'Your shoes have upon them the unmistakable loam of Marsted Meadow. It is of course the only weekend when the weaver's trefoil blooms, and Mrs Watson, renowned card-maker as she is, would surely want those choice flowers for her collection.'

'Holmes, you astound me,' I said.

He laughed, and gestured towards my favourite fireside chair. I seated myself, and we began to talk over the contents of the newspaper. Holmes leant back in his chair, eyes closed, and seemed to take no notice whatsoever of my comments. That is, until I chanced to remark on what I thought a rather unexceptional few paragraphs tucked away at the bottom of the 24th page:

'"Catcher flummoxed by 'huge rat"',' I laughed.

Holmes immediately sat upright. 'That is no laughing matter,' he said. 'Read on.'

Unsure whatever he could be about, I continued:

'"A RAT catcher has warned a rodent of hitherto unseen size may be at large. Mr Trapemhew, a pestillier of some sixty years' standing, says he has 'never seen the like' of a beast glimpsed at twilight as he passed a little-used warehouse in the Cholmwell Road. 'It was enormous,' Mr Trapemhew told the Strand's man at the scene of the sighting. 'And that's not all. It's broken two of my bacon traps.' The substantial traps shown to our reporter bore the unmistakable signs of having been sprung and the bait seized. However, the metal of each trap had then been distorted and in parts bitten through. 'It must be a hell of

a rat,' said Mr Trapemhew, who has since taken on a bacon-triggered acid shower in a bid to thwart the creature.'"

I finished and paused, waiting to hear what Holmes had to say. However, he remained deep in thought with his fingers pressed to his temples. After some moments had passed, my curiosity gained the better of me and I asked, 'Well, Holmes, what is it, man? Is there something in this rat business? What harm could there possibly be from a rat, enormous or otherwise?'

'More than you could realise,' replied Holmes, unilluminatingly. 'We must be away at once.'

'Where to?' I asked, used to Holmes' sudden calls for action.

'The warehouse,' Holmes replied.

The Cholmwell Road was only round the corner from Baker Street, so there would be no need to hail a cab.

After making a hasty breakfast – porridge, poached eggs, toast, bacon, the butcher's excellent sausages, a few fried mushrooms, kippers, a dash of kedgeree, pancakes, a good spoonful of last night's trifle, marmalade, all capped off with a pipe – we headed on our way. I bid a cheery adieu to Mrs Hudson as we passed her on the stairs, bearing off the breakfast salvers. Mrs Hudson did not return my greetings, and instead muttered under her breath as she staggered slightly beneath the weight of the trays. 'Holmes,' said I. 'Do you think Mrs Hudson is rather out of sorts today?'

'I have not noticed anything I would not expect,' replied my friend. Trusting to his powers of observation on all matters, I did not pursue the point. We hastened at a brisk walk round the corner to the Cholmwell Road, which for the most part was lined with townhouses similar to those in Baker Street. As we approached the far end though, we saw that several warehouses lay set back from the road.

'Which can it be?' I enquired of Holmes.

'All of these warehouses are clearly in regular use,' observed Holmes. 'Note the well-worn tracks. That one, though–' and he pointed to the warehouse on the far left, a distance apart from the others – 'is clearly little used. That is our warehouse.'

We drew closer, and I was about to try the door, when Holmes fell to his knees. 'Watson!' he cried. 'Look!'

I peered at the ground, and immediately saw what had so shaken my friend. Impressed into the muddy path were the footprints – of a gigantic rat. 'Good God!' I exclaimed.

'We are on the trail,' murmured Holmes, pushing open the warehouse door. Once our eyes had adjusted to the gloom, it became apparent that the vast space was empty. Or so I thought at first. Holmes, of course, knew better. He was immediately attracted to the far wall, and began tapping at it with his cane. It made a dull sound, and then, a hollow knock rang out. 'Ah ha,' said Holmes, and began caressing the wall with his fingertips. 'It must be about here...'

Our inspection was interrupted by a rude shout. ''ere!' bellowed a rough voice from the door through which we had entered. 'What's your game?' We turned to see an angry man with the look of a hired thug, accompanied by a rough and thuggish dog. 'What's your business here?' demanded the newcomer.

I was about to give him a piece of my mind for speaking to us in such an uncouth manner, when Holmes interjected.

'Is this Mulcher's Barley Emporium?' he enquired in a wheezing voice, much unlike his usual tone.

'Never 'eard of it – now clear orf,' replied our new associate in a no-nonsense manner.

'Much obliged,' breathed Holmes as he leant on my arm and staggered for the door, beneath the suspicious gaze of the watchman. Once we had rounded the corner, he straightened up and clapped his hands together, rubbing them in satisfaction. 'We are on the right track,' he said with vigour.

'We are?' I asked, confused.

'Yes,' said Holmes.

'Good-o,' I replied, none the wiser but seeing I would have to wait, as usual, for enlightenment. 'What is the next step?'

'There is nothing to be done just yet,' replied Holmes. 'I suggest you head home to Mrs Watson for a spot of lunch and call back again at Baker Street later.'

I did as Holmes suggested, but could hardly do justice to the superb rabbit casserole prepared by our cook, Ellen, for thinking what my mysterious friend could be about. As soon as luncheon was finished, I hurried back to Baker Street. Mrs Hudson was slow to answer the door and seemed somewhat put out when she saw me on the steps. She had none of her usual solicitous enquiries for my family. Indeed, she did not say a word. I could only think I had offended her in some way, and set my mind to thinking whether or not it had been her birthday lately.

A very queer sort passed by on the stairs as I headed up to Holmes' room, but, taking him for one of my friend's usual unusual visitors, I was not unduly troubled, save by his intolerable smell. I took him for a lascar, for he had a greasy ponytail, numerous tattoos and the customary garb. I knocked at Holmes' door, but there was no reply, so I took the liberty of letting myself in. The place was empty, and it seemed remarkable that the lascar should have been there without Holmes. I resolved to wait for his return and apprise him of the situation. I sat in the armchair but some time must have elapsed because I was startled to awake and again see the lascar, standing over me. 'Good afternoon, sir!' I cried. The lascar merely laughed, and helped himself to Holmes' brandy. 'You make very free with your host's provisions,' I cautioned. 'Now kindly state your business.'

'My business,' said the lascar, pulling at his ponytail, 'was simple.' All at once, the greasy mane slicked off in his hand and before me stood Holmes himself.

'Great heavens!' I cried. 'Holmes!'

'At your service,' he replied, bowing, 'and may I thank you for your solicitous care for my brandy.'

'Where have you been, Holmes?' I asked, amazed at his latest getup.

'In an opium den,' was the cool reply.

'My dear friend,' I replied. 'You know my views on these substances and the potential harm to your faculties – think of the loss to the application of human knowledge and wisdom for good! And,' I ventured, 'is it really necessary to sport so unsavoury a look?'

Holmes gave a brief laugh. 'My esteemed Watson. Thank you, once again, for your care for my welfare, but do not alarm yourself. My visit on this occasion was solely for research. I sought to hear of the legend of The Giant Rat of Sumatra.'

'The Giant Rat of Sumatra?' I repeated.

'Yes. When you first read that extract from the paper, my suspicions were aroused. I had previously heard tales of rats grown to colossal proportions, but an acquaintance in the Dutch East Indies lately told me of a folk myth that had taken hold, of a huge rat turning the unhappy population into zombies.'

'Nonsense, surely,' I protested.

'Maybe it is, maybe it isn't,' was Holmes' reply. 'I have been carrying out research of my own into the properties of certain plants that are native to Sumatra. There is a particular root – *lobotosidium* – that has become of interest to me. The properties of this root are curious indeed, for it seems that it acts on the brain of any unhappy mammal that absorbs it into its bloodstream. The effect is one of increased aggression and a sharp decline in mental reasoning. This appears to have been an established occurrence, but lately there have grown fears among the tribespeople that a rat has grown to previously unseen size and eaten a fearsome quantity of the root. In short, it has gone on the rampage, and has bitten many of the hapless people. No cure,' he added, 'has yet been found.'

'Good God, it's monstrous!' I broke out. 'And this beast, you suspect, is loose in London? But how? Did it stow away in a cargo ship?'

'That would be one explanation,' said Holmes, 'but it goes further. Consider the warehouse.'

'The warehouse?' I replied.

'Why would a rat seeking to gorge itself be at an empty warehouse?'

'Perhaps for a quiet rest?' I ventured, beginning to feel the need of one myself.

'No!' said Holmes. 'Because it was brought there, kept there and trained there until it could fulfil its ultimate purpose.'

'But what purpose?' I asked. 'Who is doing it? And why?'

'Did you ever consider the relative location of the warehouse to our present surroundings?' asked Holmes.

'No,' I said, puzzled, and then the realisation hit me that the warehouse was only a short distance behind 221B. Indeed, now I thought of it, I could just about see its dull, slate roof from the sitting-room window.

'Indeed,' said Holmes, as he saw the horrifying thought begin to dawn on my face. 'We are its prey.' Before I could panic further, he leapt up. 'Quickly!' he cried. 'Have you your trusty service revolver?'

'Always,' I replied, patting my pocket and feeling the weapon's reassuring bulk and weight.

'Then take your station in the corner over there,' said Holmes, gesturing to the far side of the room. Holmes himself sat in his armchair and picked up his violin from a nearby table.

'Holmes!' I remonstrated. 'Is this really the time?'

'Not long to wait now,' replied my friend, starting to scrape the strings with the bow. 'Now be on your guard and do not hesitate to shoot the instant you have a clear shot.'

After what seemed an eternity, I became aware of a faint scratching sound that seemed to be emanating from the chimney. Holmes looked at me significantly, and I clicked the catch of the gun. The scratching grew louder, then onto the still smouldering coals fell a huge rat, the like of which I never hope to see again. It was glowing green with red eyes and hissing violently. The heat incensed the creature, which launched itself at Holmes.

'Shoot, Watson, shoot!' he yelled, but I was horrified to realise that I had not, in fact, loaded my gun. Realising no help would come to him, Holmes thrust his beloved violin in the ghastly animal's jaws and reached to a side table for the only implement to hand. Holmes waited, poised, and as the rat shrieked its terrible advance, he swiftly stabbed downwards with a needle into its back and drove home the plunger. Holmes then leapt onto the desk, and watched coolly as the rat, pumped full of the purest Columbian cocaine, turned ever faster in circles, eyes widening. It then fell over, dead. 'It's dead,' I said, 'thank God,' and stepped forward to give the fallen foe a cautious kick.

'Watson, no!' commanded my friend, and even as I extended my toe, the horrid beast gave one last spasm and leapt for me, eyes red and evil teeth exposed. Before I could stir a muscle, there was a bang and the smell of gunpowder. Holmes had shot the brute with a gun from the desk drawer. It twitched on the hearthside rug, then lay still.

'It's dead,' I said, 'thank God,' and really went to put the boot in this time.

'Watson, you great ass,' yelled Holmes, and as I advanced the wretched creature again revived, crazed now by both the cocaine and the shot wound, not to mention the poisonous root. With a mighty spring, Holmes leapt from the desk and landed square on the rat with a cracking, squelching sound but I dared not hope too much. 'It's dead,' said Holmes, relieving me of my worries.

'Holmes, my gun – I am mortified. I don't know how to thank you,' I burst out.

'You could start by clearing up some of the rat spatterings,' remarked Holmes, trying to wrap the remains in the rug. My thoughts turned to Mrs Hudson, and I enquired of Holmes where she might be.

'Gnawing cheese, I would conjecture,' replied my friend.

'What do you mean?' I asked, taken aback by this odd remark.

'I mean,' said Holmes, 'that Mrs Hudson has no doubt fallen prey to this late beast's savage appetite.'

'Good God!' I exclaimed in horror.

'Did you not notice her both vacant and angry demeanour of late?'

'I suppose I did,' I mused, 'now I come to think of it. But what can be done? You said there was no known cure?'

'There may be something,' said Holmes, picking up a rag that had clad the lascar, while reaching into a pocket. 'At the opium den this afternoon I had a very interesting, if frustratingly stilted, conversation with a sailor who had recently returned from the Dutch East Indies. He carried with him always a sample of a plant rumoured by the local people to be effective against the bite of the rat. For a not insignificant sum, he was persuaded to part with part of his stash, and I have it here.' He drew out a dark green frond and placed it on the dining table.

'It is a leaf of the banu-banu tree,' said Holmes, 'a very rare shrub that grows in the swamps and is fertilised by pygmy elephants nudging the spores.'

Once again I was astounded by Holmes' knowledge of obscure branches of natural history and geography. 'I fancy,' continued my friend, 'that with a little manipulation it may prove to be exactly what we need.'

Holmes then fell into a fever of scientific activity, rigging up flasks, vials, flames and tubes. He placed the leaf in a beaker and set to work. A choking smoke came up, followed by an almighty bang that brought Mrs Hudson, twitching, to the door.

'Mrs Hudson!' cried Holmes, before she could object to his activities. 'Just the lady I hoped to see. I have brewed up a new type of tea and I think it would suit you excellently. Draw up a chair and have a drop.'

Mrs Hudson, looking dazed, did as my friend suggested. As she sipped a cup of the green liquid, I could see the brain fever lifting and the sense returning to her eyes. 'Just as I thought,' murmured Holmes. 'Now, Mrs Hudson, as you can see we have had an accident here with a rat and I would be much obliged if you could dispose of the remains.'

As Mrs Hudson, vastly restored, fetched a shovel and a mop, I asked Holmes what it all could possibly mean. 'How did the rat come to be here?' I demanded.

'It is quite simple,' said my friend. 'As soon as we visited the warehouse, it became apparent to me that we were dealing with no ordinary criminal. What ordinary criminal would go to so much trouble and effort with a rat? You noticed of course the strands of horse hair in the warehouse?'

I confessed I had not. 'They were not from horses transporting goods, because on sniffing and touching them it was immediately apparent they bore the traces of rosin, the waxy substance drawn over the bows of instruments to enable them to grip the strings.'

'Incredible!' I exclaimed. 'But what did that tell you?'

'It was obvious to me,' continued Holmes, 'that the rat was being kept in this isolated spot – isolated that is, except from my humble abode – and that someone was visiting it with a violin, the hairs being of the length of a violin bow. This had to me, the immediate hallmarks of a fiendish scheme of none other than the master of crime, Moriarty. Frustrated by me once too often, he no doubt sought to harm my mind in the most subtle and cruel way possible – reasoning that I would realise the slow fate to which I had been condemned with no way to effect a cure.'

'Barbarous!' I interjected.

'Indeed. He no doubt dug a tunnel between here and the warehouse, and, having heard of the rat's fame and somehow brought it here in captivity, visited it in secret and taught it to attack at the sound of a violin.'

'But what about Mrs Hudson?' I asked.

'No doubt the rat had been sent over here on a trial visit when Mrs Hudson was dusting my violin and it went for her,' replied Holmes.

'What a shocking business,' I said. 'But how can you be sure it is Moriarty?'

'Did anything strike you as unusual about the appearance of the rat, other than its size and vigour?' Holmes asked.

'Why yes,' I replied, 'it was glowing green.'

'Just so, Watson, just so!' said Holmes. 'It had been painted with phosphorous. A garish touch, no doubt designed to mock me for my detection of the Hound of the Baskervilles. But we have again bested the best and his beast and can sleep easy. I will consider, in time, what to do with my esteemed opponent.'

'Perhaps some kind of giant cat,' I suggested.

However, Holmes had shut his eyes in a weary manner and I do not think he heard me. Thus concludes the tale of The Giant Rat of Sumatra.

A Man of Books

Julia Bohanna

Ella was in her nightdress as the men moved in to butcher the garden.

In clambered the bulldozers, with cheerful shouts of men in yellow safety hats. Blades scooped out dozens of bell-faced aquilegias, bees fat as cotton balls scattered from lavender bushes. The earth was warm and pliant from summer sun; the long upwardly sloping garden had no hope of resistance.

Tears always angered father; Ella curled her arms around her mother's waist and pushed her face into a faded dress that smelt of mothballs.

'Take the girl inside,' he said. 'She's a distraction.'

Accidentally beautiful mother had called the place when it had just been the two of them. Most of the plants were from seeds dropped by birds. In father's absence, everything had been allowed to be all that it could be. Mint and thistle spread like pools of green water. They had a vegetable garden – the war effort and all that – but all they cropped were tiny potatoes and funny shaped carrots.

'It's scruffy … too anarchic,' he said, sitting on a bench in pyjamas. 'I've seen enough chaos.'

He had been ill for months. Ella was frightened by his parchment-coloured skin, the nightly ranting. But now that he was healthier, his interfering was the problem.

The digging out of the pond was the worst. No more spring frogspawn and the black commas to transform into frogs the colour of freshly washed asparagus. The evacuee children had squealed when they held them, then giggled as the frogs leapt down into the long grass, leaving behind a damp ticklish feeling in the palms of their hands that they itched at with dirty, soil-plugged nails.

Ella missed the children.

The pond was not beautiful enough for him, a soup of algae. Children had thrown in stones.

'That's how the bombs drop,' said one sad-faced boy. 'They kill people.'

At least there were no fish – just black twitching insects that rose from the silt or flitted under the warm surface of the water. Ella liked the dragonflies, like mosaic brooches until their wings quivered. Sometimes she found one dead, its distinctive colours faded by the sun – body so brittle that the legs came off in her hand.

*

'Come on, Ella,' said mother, as she stared at the bulldozers.

She stroked the nape of her daughter's neck.

'He needs a project,' she said. 'It'll be a real talking point. No more weeds.'

'We like the weeds though, Mum,' said Ella, wriggling away from puckered fingers that smelt of washing up water. 'I wish he'd never come home.'

Later, when too dark to work, the machinery hummed to a halt. In came father and tugged off his dirty boots. Mud scattered over the tiled floor.

'You must be tired,' said his wife. 'Telling people what to do.'

She was playing something complicated on the piano but several notes did not respond. Ella had been worrying at the notes when no one was around, willing them to fail. Now they sounded dull, like the thump of rabbits' feet.

'We should get this piano fixed,' said mother, closing the lid.

'I'll make it a bloody priority,' he replied. 'The girl should be in bed.'

*

Ella went upstairs, counting things stolen from her. Number one: future collecting of tiny soot coloured seeds from dried aquilegias. Number two: the prickly wild roses. She changed into the nightdress that was kicked under the bed but did not brush her teeth, running her tongue over furry enamel. Let them fall out. She'd be a gummy hag at the age of ten, an embarrassment. In six weeks it would be school. Then she could wave her arms around in dramatic gestures, telling about the monstrous bulldozers. Make a change from boring war talk. Some people couldn't let go of it, even though it was over.

*

Early next morning, a storm broke and Ella's window rattled. Outside, the walnut tree swayed. It was marked on the trunk with a red cross for destruction. The branches creaked as they thrashed back and forth.

'Like a hundred madmen watching the end of the world,' she sighed, deciding that the phrase would be written down in a section of her diary marked: *Ella's wise and clever sayings.*

Now the budding green cases would never crack in autumn and drop nut bombs onto the driveway. Another stolen joy.

In nightdress and Wellingtons, she went to look at her tree.

'It knows,' she whispered.

It felt dangerous to stand beneath it, as if it might repay her worship by tearing its roots from the ground, crushing her beneath. Her boots sucked her to the wet earth as if they wanted to plant her where she stood. She squelched over to one of the machines, touching cold metal. It looked benign without a man to turn the keys, follow orders.

Climbing back into bed, feet gritty from the inside of the boots, hair greasy with rain spray; she fell asleep and dreamt about poppies. Their bright sun-blasted faces were like the crepe paper in her art box.

*

It took weeks to finish the landscaping; people came to plant, advise and pull down the walnut tree. On the day the tree surgeons arrived, Ella and her mother went to a neighbour's house. The whey-faced indoor child, as Ella nicknamed her, spread out her marble-eyed dolls on the floor for the two of them to play. But Ella stared at the unclimbed trees in the boring girl's orchard, the unruly lawn pockmarked with daisies.

It had been hard to imagine the garden from the plans she was shown in father's study.

'Why don't you have any books?' she asked him, looking along the shelves. 'Story books.'

'Don't go in for that introspective twaddle,' he said. 'Reference books are useful but not other people's emotions.'

He always spoke to her as if she was a grown-up. She liked it sometimes.

*

Over weeks, with the digging, delivery of soil and shoring up of the layered design, something emerged. The garden was triple tiered. The only original thing left was an oak tree at the top. Plants were placed at neatly proportioned intervals, looking like shrunken heads in the brown expanses of fertile new earth.

Finally, they had an open day to show off the garden. Ella stood at the bottom of the three layers, staring at her reflection in the replacement pond. The water was clear enough to see down to the liner at the bottom. No self-respecting frog would ever let himself be exposed to a predatory world in that. People came from the village to see the spectacle of modern design. Ella sat on one of the steps, watching an ant staggering with a wood chipping three times his size. He looked like a sailing boat with legs. She juggled him from hand to hand and watched the people explore and express admiration. The second tier of the garden had the spindly trunks of recently planted trees emerging from the ground like colt's legs. It had looked better spread with springy chickweed.

*

Summer fell away and she snubbed the garden. Instead she set herself a challenge to read all the books on the shelf – even the babyish ones sent by Aunt Clare. Some were mother's, full of long words. Every evening after school, she settled into a corner, floating her hands across the top of the carpet as if skimming them over grass.

'Books have answers,' mother once said.

She intended to find the answers. Explaining the strangeness of adults, that would be a priority.

Her mother's books were hard to read. One evening, as she struggled with Nellie Dean's long-winded narration in *Wuthering Heights*, she heard her parents arguing. She tried putting her hands over her ears and then went to other parts of the house. I'll leave the front door open for the voices to escape into the sky, she thought. Then come back when they're muffled by clouds.

She climbed up the garden, patting the walnut stump like a dog's head as she passed it. How many walnuts there would have been! Finally, she reached the third tier. It was strange how father had lost interest in the garden. Now, other people came to tend it, like ugly Williams and his squeaky wheelbarrow. Did father like the order he had murdered for? Sometimes she wanted to touch his sallow face, make him look at her and explain.

She had hoped that when he was too absorbed in misery to be vigilant, something wild might establish itself in spite of the precision – a tendril of stray green perhaps. 'Nothing yet,' she muttered.

Finally, she was at the oak tree. Solid at the front, the tree was hollowed out at the back like a theatrical set.

But what was this? A path of flattened grass led behind the tree to a grey blanket secreted in the trunk. On the blanket was a small pile of books – she counted five, stacked carefully. Some had gold lettering on the spines. She could read most of the titles: *Villette* by Charlotte Bronte, *Moby Dick*, Browning's verse and two with faded writing, obviously very old. There had been someone living near the tree, a tramp perhaps.

She was excited. It had to be a man – she had never heard of a lady tramp. She put her face into the blanket and it smelled of cigarettes and oddly, her mother's perfume. Maybe it was father's hideaway, where he came to escape. Hidden depths, like Aunt Clare always said. Ella had never been close enough to him to ever take in his body smell but she knew he smoked cigars, not cigarettes. Maybe once he had smoked cigarettes – when he was the other man before the war. But there was another smell to the blanket, a sweet trace of sweat that she remembered sometimes when her mother had kissed her goodnight. But hadn't that been when father had been away? Her mother had smiled then, often looked as if she was daydreaming. Maybe she was getting confused – everyone said she was dizzy.

There was no one near the tree so she yelled hello to see if someone would appear. Then she frightened herself by imagining Blackbeard running at her with a cutthroat razor. She almost slipped running down to the house. Mother was slamming dough onto the kitchen table; father had gone for a walk. Upstairs, she flipped onto the bed and began to think about the tramp. While she wasted her life in the house, he was sitting under the shadow of the ancient tree, reading the words of novelists who were bleached bones in the graveyard.

Finding the answers.

There were some things that were too good to rush because they were rare and delicious – like the memory of eating a chocolate, or a tongueful of dissolving sugar. So she waited until the following morning before going back up to the tree. Then she was brave enough. She would ask the educated tramp what he thought of the many books he read. They would sit and discuss literature – how fine it would be to have something, someone of her own. She made sandwiches of bread and thinly rationed butter, unable to decide on the most appropriate filling. Then she wrapped them in a clean tea towel.

'Where are you going, Ella?'

Her father was coming in from the garden. He was flushed as if he had been running. He smelt of wood smoke and his eyes were glittering, for once beautiful with life.

'Just to play,' she said, feeling now that she had to get to the tree quickly.

She took the stone steps two at a time.

Next to the oak there was a telltale ring of grey ashes. In the middle, next to a rusty can, were the burnt remains of the books. She picked up the blackened *Villette*. Dozens of crisp soot stained pages came out and smeared her hands.

The blanket was gone too and with it that peculiar, uniquely adult smell.

Dance Lessons

Claire Dyer

What surprises her are the tears. These she hadn't expected. She'd expected the stomach-churning, the gripping-onto-the-armrest-until-her-knuckles-go-white kind of thing, and has shut her eyes so tight all she can see is white flecked with flashes like stars.

She's blind to what's outside the window as the plane lands at Dalaman but, as it bumps along the runway and the engines reverse thrust, she opens her eyes, looks past the large man with an unfathomable accent who's been crammed into the seat next to hers and sees the familiar mountains, the clean sky and the light, the light of Turkey. It's then that she starts to weep. Huge hot tears spill down her face and she stifles a sob. The large man with the unfathomable accent looks at her. She shrugs and attempts to smile. He smiles back. It's the first time he's done so all afternoon.

Let him think I'm crying with relief she tells herself, as she pulls her hand luggage down from the overhead locker and shuffles along the cabin. And it is a relief of sorts; relief that the waiting is almost over.

When she thinks back to the year of Tube journeys, ironing, buying groceries in Waitrose and what happened at Christmas; in some ways it seems a lifetime since she was last here. In others, the time has gone in an instant.

She doesn't question herself as to why she's here as she pays for her visa stamp or when her passport's checked at border control, or when she's waiting for her luggage to appear on the carousel, or as she climbs into the transfer car. It's too late for that now.

He'd said in one of his emails he would take her dancing, but she hasn't danced in years. She will have to learn how to do so again.

It's going to take over an hour to get there and, although the route should be recognisable, she keeps losing sense of where she is. She sees signposts flash by and the sun sets behind the mountains turning the sky blush pink, like the skin of a peach. The car rattles along, passing through the long, thin valleys lined with greenhouses made from wood and clear plastic sheeting.

When they came before, before everything, before last Christmas, her family had called them 'The Valleys of the Tomatoes' and she'd imagined the dense plump fruits hanging from the plants; generous, full of warmth; imagined their journeys across craggy landscapes to the restaurants that line the harbour. The taste of them there had been rich and sweet.

Now she's travelling alone. Like the first flight of a butterfly, her wings are still damp and creased and it hurts her to use them. She's been part of something bigger than herself forever, or so it seems. But this time, it's just her. Everything she has ever known before now has been left behind. All she's brought with her are the clothes she needs, a few books, her credit card and currency. The rest of it she's freeze-framed: the bricks of her house, each blade of grass in her garden, all the days she's spent there being a wife and mother. After all, it's the only thing she can do. After what's happened, she has no idea what else to do with it.

She is a woman, alone in her middle years, travelling to Turkey to learn to dance again with a man who has promised to teach her how; a man with eyes the colour of coal.

As the car crests the mountain road, the town is thrown below her like a carpet. Yellow lights glitter in the mild September air as they spill, a net of them, towards the sea. She knows how the fishing boats will leave early tomorrow morning, the sun turning the water silver, their wakes making shapes in it like arrowheads; they will shine like platinum in the dawn light.

The car drops her off at the villa. The garden is thick with Bougainvillea blossom, the day's heat still stored in the paving and lights dot the walls of the swimming pool, its surface smooth and untroubled. Everywhere is the sound of cicadas and down in the Old Town, the harbour is ringing with the call to prayer.

She unpacks slowly, carefully, as if staking her claim, saying to herself that she will stay here, he will keep his promise. There have been times when she's imagined him with his arm around another woman, a woman who looks like her. They are smiling into a camera and behind them the lights of his restaurant glitter and sparkle and he has also promised her, this other woman, that should she ever return on her own, he will take her dancing, he vows it will be so.

But there have been other times when she's remembered the intricate taste of the food he cooks, the gentle breeze which comes off the sea at night, the way the boats, moored at the quay, chatter to one another, men sitting on deck playing cards, the bottoms of their feet hardened, their smiles shining bright against their skin. She remembers the harbour lights, how they stitch patterns in water the colour of sapphire and it's then that she has to believe in him and in his promise to her.

When she's finished unpacking, she stands on the balcony and looks out across the bay. There is a taxi at the gate. It is yellow and rusty and makes a throaty sound as it trundles down the hill into town. Stepping out of the car, she sees him amongst the crowds on the harbour path. He turns, walks towards her, holds out his hands; his fingers when they touch hers are warm and safe.

*

I will dance, she thinks. I will spin like a dervish and forget all but what's in my sightline; the rest will be blur and whirl and fragments.

The Steersman

Robert Billing

My father, Augustus Picasso Kan, left his studio in its normal state of highly organised chaos when he disappeared.

My mother didn't tell me until he'd been away for two nights, and even then there was no urgency about her call.

'Lizzie, darling,' she said, 'is my husband with you?'

'No, sorry, Mum, I haven't seen him for over a week.'

'Let me know if you do. I think he's been getting death threats again.'

'Audrey! Have you called the cops?'

'Lizzie, I wish you wouldn't speak to me like that. Of course I haven't.'

'I'm on my way. Now.'

I grabbed my bag and legged it down to the BART station, then sprinted on board the Caltrain Superexpress. Half an hour later I was riding the elevator to the roof of a silicon chip fabrication plant in Palo Alto.

That should tell you who I am. I'm May Elizabeth Kan, Princess Tigress to the billions for whom my father's cartoons are a welcome laugh every morning.

He really did bring me up living on the roof of a factory. Ignore the details – it's a garden not a forest we have up there, and it's only four floors from the ground, not one hundred and forty nine.

Augustus used to say, 'Why draw it real, when you can draw it bigger and get bigger laugh?'

That's why everyone who reads a newspaper, or has access to the internet, thinks that we live in a pagoda on the one hundred and forty ninth floor, dress in the styles of the Ming dynasty, grow all our own food, and keep a herd of pedigree Alderney cattle, who occasionally fall off the roof with comical results.

About the time Augustus started selling his cartoons to the newspapers we had a freak tide. Part of the San Francisco subway system was flooded. In one strip Augustus put the rising sea level down to global warming. It wasn't, but he never let that get in the way of a good joke. He drew a BART train confronting a great white shark, head on, in a tunnel, then switched to the Golden Gate. He drew the bridge with the road deck completely underwater and the suspension cables just dipping below the surface, and added a startled duck.

It was about then that the gasoline dried up, and shopping stopped soon after. When the pick-out began, and you could order a specific piece of meat from a supermarket's stock, rather than ordering so many kilos and hoping you got decent quality, Augustus added a pick-out dating service to his cartoons.

He drew a strip about a young man (who looked very much like the mayor) trying to buy a girl from a pick-out shop, but because the delivery guys got confused he received an Alderney cow instead. That's when the first death threat arrived.

He framed it. It's still hanging in his studio. After that he drew a series that went on for over two weeks about the person who had written it. The humour was slightly cruel but very, very funny. The last cartoon in the series, where the perpetrator is trying to unscrew the massive clamp that holds the San Andreas fault in place, only to be killed at the last moment by a falling Alderney (the cow survives), is the one that hangs in almost every bar in the Bay Area.

The elevator doors slid open, and I let myself out onto the roof with my key.

Audrey was pottering in the garden, doing something with chilli plants. 'Lizzie, darling!' she said. 'How kind of you to come. I wonder if I should be getting worried about Augustus.'

Audrey is half Guangzhou Chinese, with a dash of Iroquois, was educated at a school for young ladies in Hong Kong when it was still British, and is as inscrutable as the Buddha.

I put my bag down. 'Tell me what happened.'

Audrey pulled off her gardening gloves. 'Let me show you. I've not touched anything.'

Augustus' studio occupied a glass-walled structure, rather like a conservatory, at the rear of the bungalow. More than half the space was taken up with bookshelves, groaning under the weight of a collection that had taken a lifetime to assemble. Beyond these were the desks, and the bank of computer screens.

Everything was switched on.

I gasped. 'You're telling me he left it like this?'

Audrey nodded.

'Augustus?' I complained. 'The father who chewed me out for wasting energy if I left the bathroom light on? Something must have happened to him. Audrey, has he been kidnapped, or worse?'

'I don't think so. He was always so careful.'

'I know, and– what's happening?'

The image on the central, largest screen changed to one of Augustus' cartoons of himself, and his voice came from the speakers.

'Welcome, Queen Fire, welcome, Princess Tigress.' Our cartoons appeared on two of the smaller screens. 'I am sad not to be here to greet you in person, but today I must be somewhere else. I cannot tell you where I am. I can tell you that the answers to your questions are where a fish in a street might see them. Queen, you are not alone, Princess, do not weep, for you have each other. We shall meet again where the cube defends the city.'

The big screen changed to another cartoon of Augustus, one in which he had exaggerated his oriental features, and depicted himself running with a rice bowl in one hand and a pair of chopsticks in the other. 'Got to go,' said the recording, 'got a dragon to catch.'

The screens blanked. 'Facial recognition,' I said. 'It was set to go off when we were both in view of the camera.'

Another cartoon popped up for a moment. 'Very good, Tigress.'

'How did he know what I'd say?'

'Voice recognition,' replied the cartoon.

The show seemed to be over, so I sat down at the desk and logged in. 'A fish in a street. It sounds like something from the Analects of Confucius. Where would a fish be in a street?'

'I don't know.'

Suddenly I remembered. 'In one of the global warming cartoons he had a fish swimming down a street, looking at another cartoon in a newspaper as it floated by. He's telling us to go through his old cartoons.'

'Looking for what?'

A bouncing chrysanthemum appeared on the screen.

'I've got a message.' I snapped my fingers in front of the flower and it opened out into an email.

'Well done, Tigress,' it read, 'Now look for the pattern.'

I began calling up cartoons, almost at random. 'What does he mean by 'the pattern'?'

Audrey found a chair. 'Themes, perhaps. The different things he talked about.'

'All right, let's start with the first ones.' I called up the flooded tunnel. 'Global warming, that's all. Second series, that's when he starts drawing us. I don't really remember this period very well, I was only about six years old. There's a joke about the deal he did to rent the roof space that I don't understand.'

Audrey leaned forwards for a better look at the screen, then laughed. 'It was Google, they put a gigantic solar panel on the roof of their building to supply power to the offices. He's telling the board of the corporation that owns the factory that a herd of cows on the roof is more environmentally sound, and much cheaper.'

I flicked to the next cartoon. One of the men in suits had asked if a cow could fall off the roof. Augustus' character replied, 'Confucius say–' and a string of Chinese characters.

Audrey translated, 'Stir fried beef very tasty.'

I giggled. Despite being three-quarters Chinese I only know a few hundred of the symbols.

The next strip showed Augustus building the pagoda, while an Alderney teetered on the edge of the roof. A man on the ground was shouting up at him, telling him that it was impossible to build anything up there, so he shouldn't be allowed to try.

I flicked on to the next series. It had quite a few frames of me at grade school, always getting the better of the other children. Then the sequence on how to run a farm on top of a building started.

He'd turned the various little everyday problems, such as plant diseases and damage by birds, into major crises which had someone jumping up and down, eyes popping with rage, while either Audrey or myself calmly found a solution. At the same time he'd worked in the changes in technology.

San Francisco itself has (in a sense) been wired for over a century. First the cable cars, then the railroads, the buses, the subway and the BART have taken advantage of centralised power. Augustus had been there when the first cars had gone on the wire, except he'd added wired roller skates and bicycles.

I found the wired bike strip, and with it some cartoons that he'd never published. I didn't understand them.

'Somebody really did build a wired bike,' said Audrey. 'Augustus claimed that they'd stolen the idea from his cartoon, and he drew these, realised that they might cause trouble, and never showed them to the editor.'

I could see why. He'd drawn the designer as a small, warty creature, sitting on a pile of stolen plans.

Instead of sending it in he'd changed the direction of the story. As the wired cars became common global warming slowed down, and the high tides, which had reached the twentieth floor of our home, receded to the eighteenth.

I was beginning to say, 'Audrey, I think there is a pattern,' when the tomato plants exploded.

The blast was more a dull thump than a sharp bang. The conservatory rocked slightly but the glass didn't break. Then there was a staccato rattle of unripe fruits hitting the windows, and finally silence.

'That must be the bomb,' said Audrey, as if she were discussing the weather. 'The man on the telephone said there would be one.'

'Audrey! Will you stop being so damned inscrutable? If there was a bomb threat why didn't you tell me?'

'I didn't want to worry you, dear, and it was outside. I saw the man put it there.'

'You did what? Why didn't you call the cops?'

'It was only a little bomb, and the tomatoes were almost over. I thought that if I ignored him he'd go away. Call the police now if you like, he'll still be there.'

'He'll still be where?' I looked around nervously.

'He had a rope to slide down from the roof. I cut the end off, so it stops half way to the ground, and I don't think he can climb up it again. He's probably still dangling, somewhere about the third floor. Will you telephone, or would you like to make some tea while I do it?'

I called the police, who called the fire department, and we watched as they came out with a massive hydraulic platform.

'I tied a knot in the rope, near the end,' said Audrey as we sipped jasmine tea. 'It would have been such a pity if he'd fallen off and hurt himself. The police would have had nobody to question.'

I tried to imagine what it would feel like to be abseiling at speed, only to be pulled up abruptly by a tightly-tied knot.

'Why?' I said. 'All right, some of Augustus' cartoons have upset a lot of people. But who in their right mind would get so angry about a cartoon – Oh!'

I stopped suddenly, realising what I'd just said.

Audrey poured more tea for both of us. 'There are plenty of people not in their right minds.'

'Is there anyone so far out of their mind that they'd kill someone over a cartoon about climate change?'

Audrey was at her most inscrutable. 'What do you think?'

'What do I think? I think–' Then I stopped, realising that the crater where the tomatoes used to be had answered my question.

She was showing her faint Mona Lisa smile. 'Just before the bomb went off you said you saw a pattern. What did you think it was?'

'Two patterns in fact. The first is the obvious one; if we are going to stop global warming we have to do things more efficiently. He was using humour to promote – no, promote is the wrong word. That would imply that he was preaching, which he never did. He was using humour to get people to think about the right questions. He drew electric roller skates, everyone had a good laugh, but they then looked seriously at wired cars.'

Audrey put down her tea bowl. 'Quite correct. And what is the second?'

'People get very angry. There's someone shouting or jumping up and down in almost every strip.'

Before Audrey could reply we were interrupted by the door chime. The monitor on the tea table lit up and showed a heavy-set, grey-suited individual holding a badge.

As I let him in Audrey found a third teacup.

'Lieutenant Green,' he introduced himself. 'That guy who was dangling from the rope had four guns with him. I'm here to make sure you are both all right, and to ask just what the heck happened.'

'I think he must have been looking for my husband, Augustus, who isn't here at the moment. Did you find out what that poor young man wanted?'

'No. I tried talking to him when the fire crew got him down, but all he'd say was that he wanted to stop Augustus stealing his world. I couldn't make any sense of the jerk. Dammit, all Augustus does is draw cartoons that give me a belly laugh every morning. We've got dozens of them pinned up at the precinct.'

'Remarkable,' said Audrey. 'I wonder why the young man was so angry.'

*

Night was falling as Audrey finished cooking our dinner. Over prawns in ginger she asked me again if I had worked out what the second pattern was. I started to say no, then realised that perhaps I did have an answer.

'Audrey, may I turn on the display?'

'Darling, of course you may.'

I clicked the switch and the tabletop became a computer screen, on which I called up dozens of cartoons, sliding them around with my fingertips, slowly building up a pattern.

'I've sorted them into an approximate order of how angry the characters are,' I said. 'What I notice is that the ones which are most directly connected with global warming have the really bad-tempered people in them.'

Audrey smiled. 'It is a useful indicator. Augustus knew that as soon as he started making an impression someone else would claim to have had the same idea first. Once they tried to kill him it would be time to move on.'

'But can't people see that he is right, and that he was first?'

'Lizzie, darling, most people can't see anything important until someone else sees it for the first time. That is why in every generation there must be a steersman, somebody who will gently guide the world in a different direction.'

'And you think Augustus is that steersman?' I let a trace of sarcasm creep into my voice, then checked myself.

'Don't you understand that he is? The cartoons make jokes about climate change, very funny ones where the sea level rises, there are lions and elephants in Antarctica and they make wine in Greenland, but once people stop laughing they ask questions. They ask the questions that need to be answered.'

'I see. But why was the man with the bomb so angry?'

'Lizzie, darling, he was simply jealous.'

'Jealous of what?'

'Jealous because Augustus had been right first. The young man had come to the same conclusions, only to find that

Augustus had got there five years previously, and had been quietly drawing cartoons, waiting for the rest of us to understand what he was saying.'

'Audrey,' I said at last. 'Did Augustus know that people would be so angry that they would come looking for him with guns?'

'He told me over a year ago.'

I interrupted. 'You mean he told you that he planned to disappear? To leave us and abandon what he was doing?'

'To leave with us, as his work here is finished. It is time to move on. The new garden is planted, the new cartoons are already on their way to the editors. People are asking the right questions about the problem, the next step is for them to ask the right questions about the solution.'

I thought about the recording. 'We shall meet again where the cube defends the city. What did he mean?'

'Try another language.'

'La Defence is a district in Paris, although I don't know what the cube is. Are we going to France?'

Audrey reached behind her and picked up an envelope. 'Let's open it and find out.' She took out a Cunard ticket wallet. 'Typical Augustus. This is so much more elegant than flying, and we could do with a cruise.'

Little more remains to be said. The strip reappeared after a very short break. In it the bomber destroyed our pagoda and reduced the tower from 149 floors to 127, a number which has much better feng shui. We stopped off in England to show the Aldernies to King Charles III, even though getting them through the Panama Canal and across the Atlantic on a junk had been fraught with disasters.

We have a new and bigger house now, on the roof of a factory that makes wired cars in the south of France. Or if you prefer the version in the strip, a pagoda on top of the Grande Arche, the huge, cubical building at the end of the Axe Historique in Paris. Our new home is, according to the strip, complete with cows, wild boar, deer and a swimming pool heated by a system of mirrors and lenses that focus the sun down the length of the Champs Elysées.

A Memory Revisited

Tahereh Zoghi

I had heard, or maybe
felt describes better,
talk of an ideal town
that remained intact,
whose features,
once beheld,
reside in the memory forever.

History is the talk of its residents –
The Welsh Marches,
playground of kings and queens;
Norman conquerors.
The Lady of Hay who built
The Castle in 1200.

My heart pinned on a sea change,
Memory opened quickly the vista
that (if I am looking for peace)
there is where it must be,
as I had once beheld
unfaded from my memory.

And as a bird finally lifting its wings,
in flying,
my heart's compass turned to that clime.
And at last, there was I
away from the vagaries of time...
in a town called Hay-On-Wye.

View from the Sea Cabbage Café

Eve Wibberley

I had mixed feelings about visiting Argentina. These people had robbed me of the man I loved. We'd been married only four weeks when Gareth was ordered to join the British Task Force being sent to liberate the Falkland Islands. It was a second marriage for both of us, but he was younger than me – too young to die.

My sister Myfanwy and I arrived by air in Buenos Aires on a foggy afternoon in late March for the start of our cruise round the Horn and up to Santiago. Her husband, Bob, was to have accompanied her but a business trip to the Far East had prevented this. I had been persuaded to take his place.

Despite my hostility towards the Argentineans, I found them warm and friendly and the tour guide interesting and knowledgeable. As my sister pointed out, it wasn't their fault the Falklands had been invaded by their military dictatorship. Although I knew this, visiting South America brought the pain and hurt sharply back into focus.

Soon it was time to join our cruise liner and during the overnight sail to Montevideo we met five Welsh compatriots and were pleased to learn there were more among the many American passengers.

Further down the coast, we called at Puerto Madryn. I had written to relatives of Gareth's in Gaiman, a small town nearby, and we hoped they had received my letter and would join us for tea. Which side of the conflict would they have supported? Although Argentinean, they are of Welsh heritage, and, among the casualties were 32 Welsh Guards including my husband.

We'd met the Lewis family in Cardiff just before the invasion, when they came over for the Eisteddfod. Myfanwy, Bob and the two of us had really enjoyed their company. But that was 25 years ago, and so it was with some trepidation that I entered the teahouse where coachloads of people were milling about finding their places. As a Welsh choir prepared for their recital, the conductor asked if a Señora Emily Lewis was present. Hearing my name, I stood up. I needn't have worried; Gareth's cousins were there and greeted us with open arms. We sat together listening to the warm voices of the choir reminding us of home. Loneliness overcame me as they closed the performance with a stirring rendition of *Land of My Fathers* and I wept for Gareth and all that could have been. The cousins were kind and by the time Myfanwy and I climbed back on the coach, I had recovered. We would correspond and they would visit me in London soon.

That night the weather worsened. Force 6 was forecast. Would this prevent the ship from putting into Stanley? I prayed hard. Part of me wanted an excuse not to visit the Islands but in my heart of hearts I knew, now I was near, that I needed to see where Gareth had died.

We awoke in the morning to find the vessel anchored in Stanley Harbour.

'Offshore islands should belong to the country nearest to them,' declared an American woman as we waited for the tender to take us ashore. *Oh, Gareth, is this what you died for?*

'Does that include Hawaii?' Myfanwy blurted out, her comforting arm around my shoulders. The woman declined to answer.

In the tender, I found myself squeezed between my sister and a tall bearded man of about my own age. With a broad grin he apologised for the jam, but I got the impression that he didn't really mind.

'That's all right,' I said, glancing up into deep brown eyes.

Somehow, in the small space, he managed to offer his hand, 'Chris is the name. And,' he added with a twinkle, 'if I'm right, you're Emily with friends in Gaiman?'

'Yes, that's right,' I was oddly flattered he'd remembered. American, I realised. 'And this is my sister, Myfanwy. What are you going to do today?'

'I'm off to Bluff Cove. I have to see those penguins!' he answered as we stood and collected our belongings ready to climb off the tender.

'Oh, so are we.' I gulped. There was a lump in my throat and I wanted to scream – *stuff the penguins – that's where my darling lost his life!*

It was a blustery, grey day but not as cold as it would have been that fateful June. Stepping on to the jetty, I filled my lungs with the sharp, clean air and felt proud, despite my heavy heart, that Stanley had been saved from Argentinian occupation. What could be more British than the scarlet phone box and double-decker bus, or the terraced Jubilee Villas built to commemorate Queen Victoria's Diamond Jubilee?

Our coach took us uphill out of the small town, 15 miles through a windswept, treeless landscape. We passed low, rounded mountains, their foothills littered with extraordinary white stone-runs left by ancient melting glaciers, rocks as large as the sheep which hid amongst them; and fenced-off wayside minefields, a grim reminder of the battle for these islands. On the way, Chris told us he had lived most of his life in the United States but that his roots were in South America.

In a lay-by, we transferred to 4x4s from local farms to descend over the rough peaty ground, covered in scrub to Bluff Cove. As if it were a race between farmer and wife, our drivers drove fast, with engines revving and gears crunching, zigzagging over the uneven soggy land, whilst we hung on as best we could. We arrived 25 bone-shaking minutes later. The beach was carpeted with down feathers and populated by Gentoo penguins gazing mournfully out over a smooth grey sea, their stench wafting inland on the breeze. I too gazed mournfully out to sea. Somewhere out there lay *Sir Galahad.* Was this where my beloved should have landed on the final push towards Stanley?

How long did I stand there? In my mind I saw the landing ship, *Sir Galahad,* anchored in the cove, crowded with troops and equipment, waiting, waiting, waiting… Should they go ashore at Fitzroy on the other side of the bay, or Port Fitzroy, another name for Bluff Cove? Such confusion fatally delayed the landing. Enemy observers reported their position and at 14:00 hours five Skyhawks came screaming overhead.

I glanced at my watch and shivered – it was two o'clock.

Round they came a second time, the whistle of the bombs and the roar of the exploding ammunition drowned the screams of the injured and dying as fire consumed the vessel; the sea became a boiling cauldron; orange flames shooting skyward and thick acrid smoke filling the air. I saw again the vivid TV news footage of navy helicopters hovering in the blinding smoke to winch survivors from the burning ship.

Why hadn't Gareth been among them?

Everything went black …

*

'Emily, Emily! Oh, thank God you're all right!' Myfanwy, her troubled eyes watching me, hugged me close.

'Where am I? What happened?'

'Don't worry. You passed out. But you're all right now. We're in the Sea Cabbage Café. Here, have some water.'

I sat up and saw Chris, the man from the ship's tender, hovering anxiously nearby and three ladies behind a counter busily preparing tea for our coach party. The delicious aroma of freshly baked cakes and biscuits filled the room.

'Chris helped me get you here,' explained Myfanwy.

'I'm so sorry. I don't know what came over me,' I murmured.

'Never mind,' said Chris, sitting opposite me, 'as long as you're all right now?'

'Yes, I feel much better, thank you,' I whispered, looking up into his kind concerned face.

Soon the room was full of chatter as our group enjoyed their food in the warm atmosphere. Fortunately, most of them had been too engrossed in the moulting penguins and other wildlife to notice me. Our guide, Colin, came over with a tray of refreshments and asked how I was. I reassured him as he sat down.

'Have you always lived here?' asked Chris.

'Wouldn't live anywhere else,' he said, 'this cove is on my land.'

'Then you were here during the war?' queried Myfanwy.

'Oh, yes! At one time the farm was briefly sandwiched between the two armies. That was pretty hairy. But the most horrendous time was the attack on *Sir Galahad* and *Sir Tristram* here…' His voice trailed off.

I gasped. I couldn't breathe. I felt I was being strangled. Quickly Myfanwy came to the rescue. 'Emily's husband was killed in that raid,' she said quietly.

The two men looked at me.

'Oh. I'm so sorry!' burst out Colin. 'I had no idea.'

Chris reached across the table, taking my hands in his. They were warm, strong and comforting. 'Look at me, Emily,' he said gently.

Looking up, I saw tears in his eyes.

'Now, take a deep breath … now another…'

Gradually I became calmer.

*

Back on board, Myfanwy, Chris and I watched from the bow as the captain directed the weighing of the anchor from the bridge. As Stanley receded from view, its lights reflecting in the darkening water, I thought of that sad day, nearly 25 years ago, when Gareth's comrades watched *Sir Galahad* being towed out to its final resting place whilst they sang *Land of My Fathers*. We moved slowly out of the smooth harbour and turned south.

'Come on,' said Chris, 'Let's go and have a drink before dinner.'

'I'll follow you in a minute,' I replied.

'Sure you'll be all right?' asked my sister.

I nodded.

Without fuss the vessel glided along the coast, past Bluff Cove. The only movement was the luminescent bow wave rippling out around the hull over the still water. I felt cold. The sea would be colder. The warm bar and companionship of Myfanwy and Chris beckoned.

Which country in South America had he come from? I wondered.

'Forget it, Emily, it doesn't matter,' it was as if Gareth were talking to me. 'Wherever he came from, he's a good man.'

'Goodbye, my love, and thank you,' I called softly into the wind. 'Goodbye.'

A Mother at the Village Fete

Pete Kimber

My mother's a compulsive organiser, and now she'd got her teeth into the village fete, she wasn't going to let go. Me, on the other hand, I like a quiet life and was shamelessly using my son to fend off her attempts to get me involved.

'Look, Mum, I've got Robert to look after and that's enough organising for me. If you want it to be another Pelham-Smith event I can't stop you, but don't expect any help from me.'

'All right then, no organising. But can I rely on you for one of the stalls?'

'Who's going to look after Robert? I've got no husband to fall back on, have I?' The 'no husband' card was always a strong one to play when mother was trying to involve me in her schemes. Strangely enough, it was she who felt guilty about my little unsupervised teenage fling which resulted in Robert's birth.

'I'll get him a place in the fete crèche for the day,' she said.

'And you'll let me choose the stall?'

She sorted through the lists she'd already assembled and passed one to me without comment.

I glanced down it looking for the stall that involved the least work. 'I'll do the White Elephant,' I offered, knowing that it would organise itself when people started to bring in all their useless, unlovely and unwanted junk.

She sighed in resignation, 'Okay I'll put you down for that. Now leave me in peace so I can make out the posters asking for more willing volunteers.'

I forbore to remind her that I hadn't started this little exchange and simply handed the list back. She pencilled in my initials and I turned back to the television.

The result of Mother's organising was a seemingly endless series of committee meetings, with tea and biscuits for the volunteers afterwards. Our small cottage was crowded nearly every evening. I tried to keep out of the way, but it was inevitable that I should hear most of the discussions.

The two youngest volunteers were from the village school and it was obvious to me that they were using the fete to get together without their parents' supervision.

'Who are those two kids, Mum?'

'You mean Jimmy and Sarah? They're sweet, aren't they?'

'You are watching them, aren't you, Mum? "Local Parenthesis" and all that.' Latin had never been my strong suit at school, but I wanted to be sure that Robert was the only unexpected event to strike our household, however indirectly.

Mum smiled, 'Yes, dear, once bitten twice shy.' Then she added, rather coyly I thought, 'Sarah says her father has offered to run the second hand book stall.'

'Well, keep those two kids busy collecting books and don't leave them alone in the hall for a minute.' I was remembering just how short my own moment of bliss had been, from a potent but inexperienced lad.

'She's been telling me about her father. He's a widower.'

When Mum mentions another man, I'm always cautious about her matchmaking attempts. 'He's young, I suppose, about my age?'

'No, Jane, it seems not. I've not asked directly, but Sarah says he's young looking and very active *for his age.*'

I was curious now. 'About how old might he be then? How old's Sarah?'

'She's 12, and a very responsible 12 as well.'

I made a few guesses and calculations: 'If he had a younger wife, he might easily have been 30 when Sarah was born, so he could be in his forties now.'

Mum smiled in agreement, 'Yes, that's what I thought, about the same age as me. Sarah said he does all the work around the house. And there seems to be no shortage of money.'

It began to dawn on me that Mum was interested. 'She's set out his stall pretty well then. And I don't mean the book stall either.' I was beginning to enjoy this.

'Don't be silly, dear, she's only 12.' Mum turned her face away from me.

'Yes but a very responsible 12,' I teased. 'Come on, Mum, she's done everything except bring you a photo.'

Mum stood up and went into the dining room to fiddle with the piles of lists and schedules on the table.

I called in to her, 'I'm sorry, Mum. Why don't you offer to help on his stall?'

She looked at me, 'Funny you should say that. Sarah said he might need some help.'

I stifled a giggle and heroically kept my face straight. With an 'I'll just slip up and look in at Robert,' I rushed from the room before the laughter could choke me.

*

Over the next few weeks, the garage gradually filled up with people's unwanted Christmas, birthday and wedding presents. On the day of the fete, Mum took Robert to the crèche while I set up the White Elephant stall. Twenty minutes later, Sarah arrived with a youngish man and they started unloading books. I wondered where her father was. He'd probably cried off and sent a younger brother or a friend. Mum hadn't turned up to help them, so presumably she knew about this change of plan.

He was quite reasonable to look at and I could see, from his oh-so-casual sidelong glances, that he liked the look of me as well. When they'd finished laying out and pricing the books Sarah wandered off, presumably to find Jimmy Brown, and he looked around. I smiled to encourage him.

He grinned back with a boyish charm and walked towards me, 'How do these things go? I've been blackmailed into this and never done it before.'

'Oh, it's really as easy as it looks. For us, anyway; most of the action will be around the children's clothes stall.' I nodded towards the tables piled with outgrown children's clothes.

'What time do they open the doors and let the hordes in?'

'You think you're joking, don't you, but hordes is what they are. The rush to that stall will be like the Sack of Rome for the first half hour, and then all the good stuff'll be gone.'

'And what time do these barbarians storm the city?'

'This tent will be opened for business at one o'clock precisely, to give everybody a fair chance.'

'So we've got plenty of time then. Some double-barrelled battle-axe was supposed to be helping me but she's not turned up.'

'She's organising the outside attractions, perhaps she'll be in later.'

'Do you know her then? To tell you the truth, I was dreading the old dragon and I'm glad she's not come. I'd rather do everything my own way.'

'Yes it's easier to work on your own isn't it?' How could I let him know the old dragon was my mother?

'Apparently she's the bossy-boots who's running this whole affair.'

I had to do something quickly and decided to try to use humour. With a wide smile and weak laugh I said, 'I'm the daughter dragon and I've been sent in to soften you up for my mother.'

He actually blushed. 'Oh my God, and I thought we were getting on so well. Tell her I'm soft enough already, will you? You've done a good job, and the heavy battalion isn't required.'

I could see he was thinking of moving away. I didn't want this so I put on my contrite, coy expression. 'Sorry, it's my fault. I should have let on sooner. I'm Jane, by the way, Jane of the dreaded Pelham-Smith variety.'

'No, no. *I* should apologise. I'm very sorry and I'd like us to start again. I'm Paul. Shall we go for a walk? I'm finding it very hot in here.' His blush was slowly dying down.

'That's a good idea. Can we go over to the crèche to see if my boy's settled in okay?' That let him know about my son before he could make any more embarrassing assumptions.

Outside, the crowds were beginning to gather, and he charmingly and lightly gripped my elbow, as if I was a delicate flower needing a strong support in all the chaos around us. The village band was tuning up, or perhaps they'd already started playing, it was always so difficult to tell with them.

We stood at the crèche barrier and looked in. Robert was playing some game with the other boys that seemed to involve lots of running around and shouting. I waved to him and eventually he waved back, but only when he thought none of the other lads could see him demeaning himself this way. I almost felt disappointed that he was having such a good time and not pining for me.

Paul must have read my expression. 'As they get older they get more independent,' he said. 'My girl's ashamed of me when I try to kiss her in public.'

His girl? Did he mean Sarah? 'Are you Sarah's father? The Sarah who collected all the books with young Jimmy Brown?'

'Who's Jimmy Brown? I thought she was out every evening collecting books with your mother.'

He *was* her father, then, some 40 year old eh? He wasn't much older than me. I remembered his question. 'Don't panic. Jimmy's a very nice lad, and my mum's much too careful, after what happened to me, to let anything like that happen to Sarah.' That let him know I had an unfortunate past, but I couldn't help smiling as I thought of Mum's disappointment, or maybe she knew and was about to try a bit of cradle snatching. 'So you're Sarah's father. I wouldn't have believed it.'

'What do you mean?'

'Sarah was very proud of you when she spoke to Mum, she said that you were very handsome, very active, very clever and very rich. She said that nobody would be able to tell how old you were because you were so good for your age. She gave you such a good reference that I think she was trying to sell you to Mum. Sarah wants to marry you off!'

He laughed, 'You're kidding!'

'I don't think so. I've got it straight from the dragon's mouth.'

'But why?'

'Who knows what kids think these days? She's just got a serious boyfriend; maybe she thinks you should get one as well. A girlfriend, I mean.'

This got him thinking, and he was very quiet as we continued our walk around the fete.

We watched the kids throwing hoops, darts and pennies on the various outside attractions, and bought misshaped cakes in the Women's Institute tent, speckled apples from the Allotment Association and raffle tickets in aid of the church tower.

When Sarah found us, we were drinking tea and eating hamburgers at the Girl Guide stand. She was out of breath and flustered. 'Where have you been? Mrs Pelham-Smith is waiting to meet you at your stall.'

'Where was she,' he snapped, 'When I needed her help to lay out the books?'

‘She was speaking on local radio, in their mobile van. Didn’t you hear her?’

‘No,’ he said even more sharply. ‘What’ve you been telling her about me?’

She smiled patronisingly. ‘It’s okay, Dad, you don’t have to be nervous, she’s going to like you.’

They were ignoring me, and I couldn’t help laughing as he shouted at Sarah, ‘She doesn’t have to like me! I’ve already got you to boss me about, I don’t need a grandmother as well.’

I stifled the laugh down to a broad smile and instinctively took his arm to urge him back to our tent. ‘Come on, it’s time we went back anyway.’

Sarah saw my hand on his arm and gave me a disapproving look, like I was trying to steal property she’d allocated to somebody else. She was right, I was. It was much too good to be wasted on my mother.

Torsten's Daughter

Hanne Larsson

Torsten's Daughter is the prologue to Hanne's first novel-in-progress, a story that aims to vindicate all those nasty things you know about trolls.

Torsten's hand reached for the keg beside him and he gulped down yet more of the moonshine; he waited for the alcohol to loosen the pain in his chest so that he could breathe again.

He remembered that look his wife had given her as if it was yesterday, the sadness of years washed away as he'd handed her the soft, mewling bundle he had found.

He'd been out that night, staring over the river, wondering how many more disappointments they were meant to endure. They would be perfect parents, but nothing worked. Even the Huldra, a species of creature not to be trusted, but whose knowledge was a last resort, had been unsure why Torsten and his wife could not have children of their own. The snow had crunched underneath his feet; even he, troll that he was, had felt the New Year's chill eating into his fingers. A small whimper had reached his ears and he'd known it was a child's and that he couldn't ignore it. She had been a beautiful baby; picking her up and carrying her home as if she was porcelain, he'd named her there in the cold, under the moonlight. Embla – one of ash.

This was what they had waited for; she was what they had waited for. He had returned home and found his wife with tears rolling down her face as she stared into the fire.

'Where did you go? You can't keep running off every time I cry,' she'd said through the tears, anger in her voice.

Torsten smiled at her reaction and handed her the blanket gently.

'What … where did you…? Who has been so generous?' she'd whispered, her customary gravel soft like river stone, as she stared at the blanket in her lap. Her face had been mist-soft, young and beautiful and he'd fallen for her all over again. His wife had looked down into the gap, into the face Torsten knew he would do anything for and had thrown the bundle at the fire.

'We can't keep THAT! It's a monstrosity; we would never be allowed. Better it is dead, that human stench will taint our house and our lives! Put it back!'

'I can't, wife. It is a child; a child is what we've always wanted. How can I put it back? It will die!'

'And when the humans come looking? They will hunt us, kill us. You know the stories; you know what's at stake! Husband, we can't keep it!'

'We will keep her. I've already named her. She is Embla.'

'NAMED HER?'

*

He poured more of the moonshine down his throat, its harshness softening as he swallowed. Good! He was aiming for oblivion from this constant repeat of an argument almost nineteen years old. Instead, another argument surfaced in his mind. He slouched further in his chair, trying to make his hulking grey form as small as possible.

'You're not going! That river is dangerous, especially now, so close to the thaw. The river nymphs are dangerous, no, more than dangerous. Cunning. They will trap you and ensnare your thoughts until you're not sure what you believe any more or what is day and night.'

'But everyone is going, Pa. Everyone. Including Uthark who's never allowed anywhere because his dad is...'

'I know what his dad is, Embla. You're still not going to that party. The boys...'

'No one looks at me like that, Pa! NO ONE! Because I'm human and not troll, and it doesn't matter what you keep saying to anyone! So why would the river nymphs be any different? They invited me especially!'

'You're my daughter, but...' he had muttered then, when she had stomped off out of earshot, her red hair glowing more than usual. '...you are different.'

They hadn't spoken since that day, skulking around each other and using polite gestures. He swigged his drink, and decided that tonight, under the bright, honest moon, there were things they needed to say to each other. Things he should have told her a long time ago.

*

Embla needed to be told the truth of the nymphs, of everything. Opening his eyes, Torsten struggled to focus on the blurry outlines of his tidy mud shack. He tried to sit up from his slouching position, but the rug kept slipping from underneath his feet. He'd stopped being angry at his wife whilst Embla was learning to walk, despite her being responsible for his daughter's burn scar. Luckily, Torsten had caught her before her hair had become too singed.

He knew his wife had tried, had tried to love this child who wasn't theirs.

Torsten could see how much pain she was in for all her trying, especially round the eyes and her furrowing brow. She would be jolly and warm, all the things a mother should be: but her look betrayed her. Her skin darkened from a lovely warm grey to almost coal when she picked the child up. Torsten couldn't understand how she couldn't accept their daughter. Once, Embla had scraped her arms whilst climbing a tree; she had run off to bandage herself rather than turn to her mother.

It had been a relief when Torsten had found the runes spelling out his wife's intentions on the table; he hoped her journey would lead her back here one day. He missed how she would nuzzle into his neck as she had used to when they had been courting, and then as newlyweds. But as each season turned into another, his skin forgot how his wife had used to soften it. Embla became HIS daughter. He only remembered his wife's name at maudlin moments like this. She had known that he would not leave the foundling, and had not made him choose.

*

He got up on wobbly legs, shivering, and stoked the fire, wrapping himself in the moss blanket Embla had stretched and stitched for him. The cold was harder to push from his body, his joints taking an age to loosen. Age was creeping up on him. One day soon Torsten would stare straight at the sunlight and turn to stone, as his parents had done. You lived till you couldn't hide from the sun quick enough. He hoped his daughter would understand that, when the time came.

The elders had fretted over his decision to raise Embla alone. Torsten had shaken his head at their suggestions for another marriage. He could see the fear in the candidates they had put forward; no one wanted to be tainted with a child like her. A foundling. A human foundling that a troll fire had marked. She would be bad news; Torsten must be cursed by the Moss herself.

But he loved this wisp of a thing; all fiery hair and pale skin that burned in direct sunlight. She might not look like a troll, but she had the heart of one. He had been smitten as soon as he'd picked her up that night by the river and stared into her grey eyes that changed colour with the weather. It was the pair of them against the world. Or it had been.

One last swig of the moonshine and he marched towards the door and out into the night. She needed to move back home. The village was beginning to talk.

He glanced upwards. Honesty's moonlight, he thought, stumbling towards Uthark's house and keeping to the shadows. But perhaps he didn't need to tell her everything tonight – he could start by apologising and explaining why the party wasn't a good idea for her.

'EMBLA! Come here – I need to talk to you!' His voice bellowed out in a gruff as he reached Uthark's house. 'You need to come home! Embla!'

His vision blurred as the door opened and a shape stood in front of the fire. 'Let me see her!'

'Who, Torsten? Your daughter? Embla isn't here – she left hours ago, said she was going to the river.'

'The RIVER?! Why didn't you stop her? You're lying, stop hiding her! Let me see her!' He tried to push past the youth and into the house itself.

'She's not here! By Moss, I promise you.'

Torsten sank down onto his creaking knees, and didn't move. He could wait here for the summer sun, and turn to stone then. 'I need to find her ... I need ... not the nymphs. Not her. Why ... I need ... how can I get her back?'

'Come in, Torsten, it's time someone in this village helped you with that daughter of yours...'

A Father at the Village Fete

Peter Kimber

My twelve-year-old daughter looked across the kitchen table at me with that winsome, longing look that so reminded me of her mother. She was turning on her twenty kilowatt charm and I waited, with some trepidation, for what was to follow.

'All the other kids have got their parents doing something for the fete. Why can't we do something?'

Oh no! I thought, it's an *all the other kids plea.* In fact, Sarah was pretty good and rarely used it. She knew that as a widower bringing a child up alone, I simply couldn't match the efforts of other parents, and I knew that when she did use it, she really wanted what she was pleading for.

She noticed my hesitation, and taking it as a sign of weakness, played her strongest card. 'I'll get everything ready. All you'll have to do is to spend a Saturday afternoon at the fete instead of watching football on TV.'

I was weak and agreed, but then I'm only a man and no match for the charms of a lovely young girl. *Well I'm her father aren't I? If I can't say she's charming and lovely, who can?*

Sarah arranged for me to help a woman called Mrs Pelham-Smith to run the bookstall in the main tent. This woman was also the organiser of the whole thing and sounded just the type that I normally keep well away from.

Sarah worked really hard over the next few weeks and the growing piles of books in the garage soon forced me to leave the car on the drive. She really seemed to look forward to the evenings she spent out collecting books. I assumed Mrs Pelham-Smith had somehow managed to inspire her with a good Christian work ethic, which anyone of that name would have in abundance.

On the morning of the fete, Sarah helped me to get the books to the tent, but she disappeared as I laid them out on a couple of tables. Of course, Mrs Pelham-Smith was much too busy *organising* to help with such a mundane task but the general camaraderie in the tent made it seem light work. The woman on the white elephant stall next to me was youngish, with attractive hazel eyes, light brown hair in soft curls, a clear country girl complexion and a ready smile. I didn't give her much attention but I felt that it was only civil to start up a conversation. She spoke softly with a charming hint of a Berkshire accent and had the good sense to laugh at my jokes. We got on like a house on fire and I discovered that her name was Jane and she was a single parent with a boy in the fete crèche. When I complained about the absence of my helper she looked at me sheepishly and admitted that Mrs Pelham-Smith was her mother.

We soon finished preparing our stalls and, as they weren't due to open until the afternoon, I suggested a walk. Jane agreed, provided we went to the crèche first to make sure her boy was happy. The outside attractions were now all going strong and the crowd was beginning to grow. I gently gripped Jane's elbow as we walked, just in case she slipped on the trampled grass, you understand.

At the crèche we found that Jane's boy was having a whale of a time, so much so in fact that he could spare no time for his mother. Jane looked so dejected at this that I couldn't resist telling her what other disappointments she might expect in future.

‘As they get older they get more independent.’ I said, ‘My girl is ashamed of me when I try to kiss her in public, she says that men shouldn’t do that.’

Jane looked at me more closely, ‘Are you Sarah’s father? The Sarah who collected all the books with young Jimmy Brown?’

‘Who’s Jimmy Brown? I thought she was out every evening collecting books with your mother.’

‘Don’t panic. Jimmy’s a very nice lad and my mom’s much too careful, after what happened to me, to let anything like it happen to Sarah.’ Jane smiled as she mused, ‘So you’re Sarah’s father. I wouldn’t have believed it.’

‘What do you mean?’

‘Sarah was very proud of you when she spoke to Mum, she said that you were very handsome, very active, very clever and very rich. She said that nobody would be able to tell how old you were because you were so good for your age. She gave you such a good reference that I think she was trying to sell you to Mum.’ Jane was laughing as she went on, ‘Sarah wants to marry you off!’

I didn’t think it was so funny, it’s a bit much when your daughter thinks you’re only fit to marry a grandmother. I was very quiet as we continued our walk around the fete.

The village band was playing a selection from the *Mikado*, or was it from *Carousel*? It’s always so difficult to tell with them. We watched the kids throwing hoops, darts and pennies on the various stalls, we bought mis-shaped cakes from the Women’s Institute, speckled apples from the garden produce stall and raffle tickets in aid of the church tower.

We were drinking tea and eating hamburgers when Sarah found me. She was out of breath and flustered, 'Where have you been? Mrs Pelham-Smith is waiting to meet you at your stall.'

'Where was she,' I retorted, 'when I needed her help to lay out the books?

'She was speaking on local radio, in their mobile van. Didn't you hear her?'

'No,' I said, and then added sharply. 'What've you been telling her about me?'

She smiled patronisingly, 'It's okay, Dad, you don't have to be nervous, she's going to like you.'

I saw Jane beginning to laugh again as I shouted at Sarah, 'She doesn't have to like me. I've already got you to boss me about. I don't need a grandmother as well.'

Jane was smiling broadly as she took my arm and pulled me towards the tent. 'Come on,' she said, 'it's time we went back anyway.'

Sarah looked aghast at Jane's hand on my arm and we all walked towards the tent. Of course, when we got there my so-called helper had disappeared again and that suited me very well. Jane went to her stall and Sarah and I went to ours.

When we were alone Sarah whispered to me, 'You know she's got a baby and she's not married, don't you, Dad?'

I pretended to be shocked and replied, 'She never told me she had a baby.' And when Sarah looked smug I added, 'She said it was a boy at school. We've been to see him, he looks like a nice kid.'

When the tent opened the villagers rushed in looking for bargains, there were big crowds around the children's clothes stall all afternoon and it was entertaining to watch the mothers pushing and shoving to get to the front. There was a steady stream of villagers walking around the tent with no definite purchase in mind. Some of these stopped at my stall and disarranged the books. The afternoon passed pleasantly enough, as I chatted to old friends and tried to show Jane that all the things Sarah had said about me were true. I even sold a few books.

Sarah appeared again as I was packing up the books. She had a young lad with her who I assumed was Jimmy Brown. He was the first boy that she'd ever let me see, so I guessed that it was serious. They helped me to carry the books out to the car, but all three of us were too embarrassed to say much and the resulting silence only increased our embarrassment. Finally, to my relief, Jimmy had to leave us to go back to his parents.

Sarah and I got into the car to go home. 'Jimmy seems a nice lad,' I said, trying to get a conversation started. 'Have you known him long?'

'Yes, simply ages, ever since the school trip. He helped me to get all the books for your stall.'

'Why didn't you tell me you were going out with him in the evenings?'

Sarah then, with the naivety and arrogance of a twelve-year-old, showed me why I was right to love her so much.

'I didn't want you to worry about being left on your own when I get married,' she said.

Sarah the schoolgirl was changing into Sarah the young woman who worried about her old dad. She wanted to be sure that he was settled and married before she left home.

That's why she had schemed and worked so hard over the last few weeks, trying to fix me up with Mrs Pelham-Smith. Maybe she'd nearly got it right. After all, the idea of marriage had crossed my mind that afternoon too, but not to Mrs Pelham-Smith.

Churned with Love

Eve Wibberley

Churned with Love is the caption for a butter advertisement but it's a good description of what happens to men and women when they fall in love. Mixed up and agitated. Look at Lucy sitting in front of her computer, hands poised over the keyboard, grinning inanely and gazing starry-eyed at the screen. From here I can't see what program she's using, but at a guess it's not Excel. Whoops, here comes trouble. No, she's quick enough to bang a few keys as the boss walks by. Her face is scarlet and she knows it.

It's time to go home to my dogs and I meet her in the cloakroom where she's carefully adjusting her make-up and brushing her long fair hair.

'Where are you off to then?'

'Never you mind,' she replies as she flounces off.

She's right. It's none of my business. I'm old enough to be her mother and she's unlikely to confide in me. In my head I can see my tall, elegant mother saying, 'Have you told me everything? It'll all end in tears.' I hate to admit it but she was right. She would know wouldn't she? She managed to get through several lovers in her lifetime. I almost gave up counting after I left home. 'Tis better to have loved and lost than never to have loved at all,' she'd titter, but I do feel she overdid it. Was it worth the bitter recriminations and traumas at the end of each relationship or the despondency and misery during the lull before the start of a new one?

*

The first love in her life that I knew about was Arthur, my father. Tall and good-looking, every woman's dream, it seems. Apart from the ladies, he had another love – whisky. He was a salesman and whenever possible mother sent me out with him presuming he wouldn't go to the pub with a small child in tow. But crisps and pop were sent out to me in the car. He died young, but not before he'd landed a few black eyes on mother whilst in his cups. She sent him packing. Some people muttered that she was enough to 'drive anyone to drink'. Perhaps there was some truth in that. She loved shopping and was forever demanding money. My aunts had never seen anyone with so many pairs of shoes. I thought it was normal and confess to a passion for footwear myself. She and Imelda Marcos had much in common.

Harry, an American soldier in his well-tailored uniform, with silk stockings to woo the girls and sweets for the kids, was next on the list. I described him as 'tall with a drawl', which annoyed mother. He didn't live with us, but visited frequently. He'd come roaring up to the house in his jeep and leap out over the side into my mother's open arms. With a fistful of chewing gum, I was sent out to play and told not to come back till bedtime. I heard my friend's mother, arms akimbo, head nodding knowingly in my direction, tutting to her neighbour over the fence: 'They're overpaid, oversexed and over here.' Something like that had been said on the wireless but I couldn't think what it had to do with me. Harry disappeared after a few months and we never heard from him again, so I lost my extra sweet supply to barter with at school and mother was miserable once more.

Not for long. Harry seemed to have given her a taste for men in uniform but I was startled when the police car pulled up outside our house. Mike must have started life somewhere in Ireland judging by his accent, but I have no idea where mother met him. With a wink, he told me she was going *to help him with his enquiries.* Sometime later, Mike moved in, but as he worked shifts I didn't see him very much, thank goodness. I was now in my teens and if mother happened to be out when he came home, it was very obvious that he wanted me to *help him with his enquiries.* I soon learnt to nip out of the back door when I heard his key in the lock. Whilst I was away at secretarial college, Mike was implicated in a scandal and he had left by the time I came home for the summer vacation. Years later, I discovered that he, with several of his colleagues and some ladies of the night, were accused of using the prison cells at the police station for activities other than the retention of criminals. It was all hushed up, but Mike left the police force and presumably, without his uniform, he lost mother as well.

When I started work, I lived in a hostel and went home occasionally at weekends. One Friday evening I got the shock of my life. My cousin's husband, Tom, had seemingly left his wife and taken up residence with us. Only temporarily, I was assured, till he could sort things out at home. He was an Air Force officer and another man who couldn't keep his hands to himself. In time the 'temporary' became 'permanent' and my cousin divorced him. Mother and Tom eventually married till death did them part.

Going through her papers after the funeral, I came across my parents' marriage certificate which was dated two years after I was born. I was also surprised to learn that she'd been married previously. So there was another love I never knew.

What a life. Is it any wonder I decided never to declare 'I do' to anyone and bought a dog instead? Mind you, I've had my moments of weakness, but my beloved dogs have always seen them off.

Poems of Poverty and Wealth

Charles Whittaker

Band of Hope

See, the ragged army climb
the barren hills, above the fertile earth
and grey slated sandstone church.
Exiled from the village of their birth,
do they see the yellow roadside flower,
the lichen on the milestone, as they trail
through wooded vales, their countenances sour,
set hard against the bitter brow they scale?

Not muskets in these hands, no sharpened sword.
Defeated now, their dignity is forfeit
in the spades, the hoes and hammers left behind.
Their homes and smallholdings at the master's word
were taken back, like playthings, for his profit.
The bleak sun in the west is less unkind.

Desertion

Sandalled feet along the dust-filled road,
edge towards a bare horizon;
no tents come into view,
no red crosses, no packages, no food.

Crawling across the earth, fiery red like fresh blood,
over children's rib stretched corpses;
burning hands and knees,
my wife is frail; no food.

We are alone, forgotten and unloved.

Empty Trough

Woe to those ensconced so snugly in Zion
and to those who feel so safe on the mountain of Samaria...
... they will be the first to be exiled;
the sprawlers' revelry is over.
(Amos Ch.6 v.1 and 7)

We were successful once; the champagne toast
in plush hotels at a hundred pounds a bottle.
Our glass walled riverside apartment
looked out across the towered city,
mirroring the place we slaved all day.
No longer in green awareness do we walk
the elegant footbridge to St. Paul's
or drive the Lamborghini
at the weekend out of town.

The trough is emptied, like our desks;
the padded chairs and Vaio laptops
confiscated now, and stored
awaiting our inevitable rebirth.

The pay-off package should be enough
to scrape along. I'll put the penthouse flat
in the wife's name just in case,
then lease it to a pious politician
trying to unravel the financial mess
we left. Then, as Del-Boy rightly said
'The world's your lobster',
probably on a Caribbean isle,
with a little more champagne.

Rocky Road

Judy Hodgetts

'Whoa!' Ben yelled, turning round in his seat to see where he was. 'How did we get to be in a spacecraft?' He pinched his arm to check he wasn't dreaming, but it definitely hurt. He screwed his eyes tightly shut, but when he opened them he was still in the spaceship, sitting next to his best friend, Charlie.

'How did we get here?' Charlie shouted, frantically looking round the tiny cabin.

'I don't know,' Ben said, trying hard to think back. 'We were playing Star Wars in the playground ... and then Jack joined in.' He gulped as he thought about Jack, and his stomach churned with a familiar squishy feeling. Jack had started calling him names – again, and had pushed him over. In front of his friends. Ben had skidded across the concrete before hitting his head on the wooden fence. It had hurt and he'd started to cry, even though he'd tried hard not to. Jack and his friend Toby had yelled 'cry baby' before running off.

'Oh, yes,' Charlie replied, but his attention had moved to the huge computer keyboard in front of them. 'This is cool!' he said, his eyes opening so wide Ben thought they might pop out. 'Look at all this!' he added, grabbing Ben's sleeve and bouncing up and down in his wheelchair. He held his fingers over the keyboard. 'I wonder what all these buttons do.'

It took Ben's mind off feeling scared. This was what he loved – computers. 'Let me see...' He studied the keyboard closely before moving things around on the touch screen. 'Clicking on this will make us go faster.'

Charlie jabbed at the screen and the spacecraft zoomed forward. 'Wahoo!' he shouted.

Ben laughed as his stomach somersaulted four times in a row. 'And by pressing this–'

BANG!

The spacecraft shuddered as it was pushed to one side. 'What was that?' Ben gasped, peering out into the darkness. 'Oh, no!'

'It's Jack!' Charlie shrieked. 'He's in a spaceship with Toby – and they're ramming us.'

BOOM!

Ben grabbed hold of Charlie's arm as the spacecraft juddered again.

'Do something!' Charlie yelled, his voice trembling.

'Okay, okay,' Ben replied, trying to concentrate on the computer. 'I think if we press these two keys together, and then this one–'

'Or this one?' Charlie suggested, his fingers hovering over a bright red button.

'No! That's–'

The spacecraft was jolted from behind, and Charlie lurched forward, his hand landing on the key.

'–the ejector button!' Ben screamed as the roof slid open and they were hurtled into space. He managed to grab hold of Charlie's wheelchair with one hand, and eventually they slowed down, but all they could do was float around aimlessly.

Jack's spaceship drew alongside them. 'Ha, ha, ha!' His face twisted in a howl of laughter. 'What you gonna do now?'

'Yeah!' Toby added. 'How you gonna get home?'

Ben started to cry, huge tears sliding down his cheeks.

'Cry baby! Cry baby!' Jack and Toby sang, before their spaceship roared away with a loud vroom.

Ben wiped his eyes on his sleeves. 'What *are* we going to do?' he asked Charlie.

'I don't know,' he replied, 'but hold onto the back of my chair – and don't let go!'

Ben clung on tightly as they drifted slowly through the blackness, with only the occasional star twinkling through the gloom. He fought back hot tears.

'Hey, look!' Charlie shouted, pointing to the arm of his wheelchair. 'These buttons weren't here before.'

Ben leaned over his friend's shoulder. 'That's funny,' he said. 'See what happens if you press the yellow one.'

'It's started an engine!' Charlie said. He shrugged at Ben. 'I didn't even know my wheelchair had an engine.'

'And what about the green button?' Ben asked, excitement rippling through him.

'Whoa – turbo boost!' Charlie cried as orange flames blasted out of the wheels, shooting the boys forward so fast Ben nearly fell off.

They whizzed in between asteroids and twinkling stars, dodging round comets with brightly coloured tails.

'There's Earth!' Ben shouted, pointing to a distant swirl of greens and blues.

'Awesome!' Charlie replied. 'And what's that planet?'

Ben looked at the orb hanging just below them. It was streaked with shades of vivid reds and purples. 'I don't know,' he replied. 'I don't remember it from any of my books.'

'Let's go and find out then!' Charlie yelled, guiding his wheelchair towards it.

They landed with a bump, showering dust everywhere. Ben coughed and spluttered, wiping dirt from his eyes. 'Ooh,' he said slowly. 'This looks weird.' He stared up at the mountains either side of them, which stretched as high as he could see. Jagged rocks were overhanging the narrow path they'd landed on.

'Yes,' Charlie agreed. 'I've never seen red or purple rocks before.'

'Me neither,' Ben said. 'And, listen! They're humming!'

'That's not humming,' Charlie said, 'it's moaning and groaning – the mountains aren't happy! Let's get out of here!'

'Okay!' Ben jumped on the back of the wheelchair and Charlie pressed all the buttons, but nothing happened.

'Oh, no!' Charlie groaned.

'I don't believe it,' Ben said, hopping off. 'Shall we go and see if we can find someone to help us?'

Charlie wheeled his chair forward and Ben walked beside him, although this wasn't easy with his knees knocking so much. The humming grew louder and boulders started to tumble down the mountainsides, landing around them. Ben walked nearer to Charlie, grabbing hold of his arm.

A loud thump behind them made the ground shake and shudder. 'I think someone or something just landed,' Ben whispered.

'Please let it be a rock,' Charlie answered, his voice shaking.

Ben held his breath and the boys turned round slowly.

Two aliens were towering over them, each with four of their six arms folded across their chests. They had purple bodies, and one had green slime oozing out of his nose. The other had orange pus dripping from his eyes. Their skin was crinkled like an old apple and the smell of rotting fish crept up Ben's nose, making him feel sick.

The boys shrieked together. 'Arrrrgh!'

The aliens covered their ears with two of their hands, shaking their heads from side to side and groaning.

Ben cupped his hands round his mouth and yelled to Charlie, 'They don't like the noise!' He glanced up at the mountains. 'Keep screaming!'

'Arrrrgh!' Ben and Charlie shouted louder. Ben hoped his plan would work, but his heart was hammering so much he thought it might explode. And his legs felt as if they were made from jelly.

The noise started to bounce off the mountains, just as Ben thought it would. It crashed and echoed round the valley with a deafening roar. The aliens clamped all six of their hands over their ears, before shaking their heads and shouting loudly at Ben and Charlie. And then, to Ben's amazement, they ran away.

Ben leaned against Charlie's wheelchair. 'That was scary,' he panted. 'I hope they don't come back.'

'Me, too,' Charlie said. He held out both his arms. 'Look how I'm shaking.'

'We need to think how we're going to get home,' Ben said. 'Shall we try the buttons…' He stopped talking and lowered his voice. 'Look over there! What's that, moving behind those rocks?'

Charlie gulped. 'More aliens?'

Ben nodded. 'We need to find somewhere to hide – and quickly!'

Two figures started running towards them, shouting and waving. Ben shook his head. 'They're not aliens,' he told Charlie. 'It's Jack and Toby!'

Jack and Toby stopped in front of them, and Jack put his hands on his hips, glaring at them.

Ben swallowed hard. 'This is nearly as bad as the aliens,' he whispered to Charlie.

'Yes, but we frightened them away!' his friend replied.

Ben puffed out his chest. If he could scare aliens, he wasn't going to be worried about Jack anymore. 'What are you doing here?' he asked.

'We came to have a look round,' Jack replied, 'and our stupid spaceship broke down.'

'And we were hiding from the aliens,' Toby added. 'We were really frightened.'

Jack scowled at him. 'And now we need a lift home,' he said.

Ben shrugged his shoulders. 'We lost our spacecraft, remember? We're stuck as well.'

Jack carried on staring, but his bottom lip started to wobble. He fell onto his knees and started sobbing. 'I want to go home,' he cried.

Ben's mouth dropped open.

Charlie whispered, 'Cry baby,' just a little too loudly and Ben giggled.

'You were so brave scaring them off,' Jack said in between sobs. 'Toby and I just hid.'

'Come on,' Ben said to Jack, helping him up. 'Let's take a look at your spaceship.'

Jack and Toby both sniffed loudly as they walked to the craft, which was hidden behind the rocks.

'It won't start,' Toby said. 'These buttons keep flashing and we don't know what it means.'

Ben peered at the computer screen, working things out in his mind. 'I think if we press these three keys together, followed by this one and this one...' He worked quickly and then pressed the ignition button. The spaceship fired up, the loud brrrm of the engine making them all jump.

'Thank you, Ben,' Toby said, smiling at him.

'Yeah, thanks,' Jack said sullenly. He turned away, muttering, 'You're always so clever with computers.'

Ben tapped Jack on the shoulder. 'Is that why you're so mean to me?' he demanded.

Jack turned round and stuck his hands in his pockets, staring down at the ground. 'Mum says we don't have enough money for a computer...' He poked at the dirt with his shoes. 'So I don't really know how to use the ones at school.'

Ben thought about the new laptop he used at home. 'If you want to come round to mine after school, I could show you?' He suggested this quietly, not sure if Jack would laugh. 'Go to a geek's house for tea? No way!' he would probably reply.

'Oh!' Jack looked up at him. 'Really?'

'And I've got the new Star Wars game on PlayStation,' Charlie added. 'You and Toby can come and play it with me and Ben.'

Jack and Toby beamed at the two boys. 'Thanks, I'd love that,' Toby said.

'Me, too,' Jack added as he high-fived Ben.

Ben checked the clock on the console. 'Lunch break has just finished. We need to get back to school!'

*

Ben opened his eyes and rubbed his head. Why was he sitting on the ground with Miss Wilson, his class teacher, kneeling next to him?

'Thank goodness you're all right, Ben,' Miss Wilson said, helping him up. 'You knocked yourself out.'

'Are you okay?' Charlie was peering at him.

'Yes, I feel great!' He beamed at his friend.

Jack was watching from across the playground and Ben walked over to him. 'Don't ever push me again,' he said.

Jack blinked several times. 'No, Ben. And I'm sorry.' He smiled nervously. 'Is it still okay for me to come round to your house?'

'Yeah,' Ben replied with a grin. 'I'll see you later.'

Passiflora

Hanne Larsson

Dear Maleficent,

I hope this letter finds you busy with work. What a peaceful and tidy place your tower must be compared to the explosion of pizza boxes and ice cream tubs that has become my cottage. I felt obliged as your friend to write to you before you heard any of the rumours linking you to evil-doings and pranks.

As I previously mentioned, I've been keeping my eye on this blonde slip of a girl living in dismal conditions in her stepmother's house as an opportunity for new business. One morning, the mice in the kitchen helpfully told me that her stepmother had forbidden her to attend the ball held in honour of all the land's noble ladies. I grabbed my chance, knowing that there is much to be said for making an entrance. Her mouth gaping and a single tear falling as I materialised in front of her, sparkles and all, told me I'd succeeded.

In time-honoured fashion, I promised she would be allowed to go to the ball, as long as she left before midnight. Dearest Mally, my heart did a little somersault when she nodded, and I gave her a list of items that would need to be ready the evening of the ball.

*

The stepmother and her hideous daughters had left hours before I showed up that evening (well, the handbook does say that the belle of the ball has to be fashionably late, which gives me room to do my job. I do have to think of repeat business). Such was the plan anyway.

I am great at fairy godmothering, been doing it for years. I have a reputation to uphold and reams of references from other down-and-out girls who I've turned into princesses and saved from sleeping sickness, dragons or evil queens. So I honestly don't know why, that night, nothing worked. Of course everything is hunky-dory now that the Fairy Council have banned me from using magic for business.

First, the pumpkin. Normally this turns into a beautiful white carriage complete with muted gold wheels and adorable lace curtains in the windows. It was the strangest feeling, a bit like that incident in '83 when the dry rot got into that batch of school broomsticks (kids + fire + flight = bruised and crying children), you remember? Only this time it was the wand itself. Fizzling, whimpering and a sputter of light flew out, turning the pumpkin into a marrow. Hideous vegetable, the marrow, I'm sure you agree. And once magic has been applied, you can't use it for anything other than making bland soup.

The girl, bless her heart, managed a huge smile when I turned to look at her. Onwards and upwards I thought; a spare carriage should be easy to find.

The mice were standing up, as if eagerly awaiting their human transformation. The wand felt less sick this time around, certainly there was less coughing and spluttering, but the results weren't quite right. One of the footmen turned out magnificently – clipped ash blonde hair, standing smartly to attention in his blue uniform, but the other! The other was a monstrosity of halves, one gleaming, the other furry and twitching. He would have to go to the shelter.

Her smile had faded, replaced by a biting lip and a look of panic in her eyes. I gave her my most confident smile, pulling out the back-up wand from my bag, but I was sure my trembling hands were giving me away.

On the basis of the previous 50% success rate, I figured a new wand would mean 100%. Then all we would need to do was find another mouse, a carriage and I could send her off to meet her prince.

Sounds simple, doesn't it, especially with such an easy trick of turning one four-limbed beast into another?

However, the lizards were a lot less co-operative than the mice. The wand felt fine in my hand, with a nice weight, but as I twirled it round for the final cast, it splintered! The whole thing cracked into fragments, the largest of which flung itself against the girl's head, knocking her unconscious.

In retrospect, her unconsciousness saved me losing face whilst on THAT embarrassing phone call. You must be the only one of us that has never used the FAA and asked for magical assistance and tow-aways. Inevitably, you always spot at least one of the fairy grandmothers sniggering as they put your spells right. And five of them turned up! FIVE! I've broken Merry's record!

Well, the short and long of it is that the girl got to the ball, but beyond fashionably late. The Prince had already picked his belle. I had failed.

Now it turns out that that undernourished blonde isn't as air-headed as she looked and is suing for malpractice! I am currently suspended from using magic for business purposes, and frankly I am a tad bored. There's only so much tea to make and pizza to conjure up (and the kitchen mice have refused to tidy up)…

You have always been a good friend to me, so any thoughts on what I ought to do now?

Your loyal friend, Flora

Maleficent sniggered to herself as she reread the letter for the second time. Passiflora (how she hated nicknames!) had always been the naive one, and Maleficent had been going stir-crazy with nothing but the crow and the dragon for company. With her powers still greater than anyone else's on the Fairy Council, nothing had posed much of a challenge since that Sleeping 'Beauty' affair (and that had been against three), so she tended to lay low.

Passiflora's excitement over her new client had made sabotaging her spells an irresistible prank. Maleficent supposed she ought to reply to the poor sap and make all the right friend noises, perhaps even find an ally in her; yes, that would be just the challenge she wanted.

Maleficent grinned darkly. Droves of do-gooder fairies practically skipped out of the college every year. They should thank her for providing them with opportunities to 'save the day'.

This piece, as Passiflora's Suspension, was performed at a Liar's League event in March 2013.

Bamako

John Shepherd

You may own a bigger house, you may drive a cooler car.
You may earn a lot more money, be richer by far.
You may write better poetry, you may be a star.
But I've driven a Nissan Micra to Bamako.

I'm not the first to drive there and I'm sure there will be more.
But most of them will get there in a brand new 4 by 4.
Not a 20 year old banger with our logo on the door.
I've driven a Nissan Micra to Bamako.

My friends thought I'd not make it; I didn't have a chance.
A couple of them said that I'd never get to France.
I wish I'd had the confidence to bet in advance.
I've driven a Nissan Micra to Bamako.

I've been through a place so arid dead camels wouldn't rot.
Not even bloody vultures would venture to that spot.
And as for the heat – my God was it hot.
I've driven a Nissan Micra to Bamako.

I've driven through a minefield, dug the car out of the sand.
Pitched my tent where hyenas might gather in a band.
I've peed in urinals made of camel dung and
I've driven a Nissan Micra to Bamako.

I've been stopped by more police than they've got in the Met.
Been injected 'gainst diseases didn't know that you could get.
If there is a harder drive I haven't found it yet.
I've driven a Nissan Micra to Bamako.

I've slept with a scorpion under my bed.
A funnel web spider not far from my head.
And as for the toilets – that's better not said.
I've driven a Nissan Micra to Bamako.

I have a small confession I have to make to you.
My target wasn't Bamako, I aimed for Timbuktu.
But there were bandits and floods, so Bamako will do.
I've driven a Nissan Micra to Bamako.

Fur Coat and French Knickers

Eileen Dickson

A silver moon slung low in the night sky and grey shapes moved beneath it, long blunt muzzles raised upwards. Howling pierced the air and small animals took fright, scuttling away into the undergrowth.

'That's better, lads, but you need to really open those throats – show you mean business.' The Wolf looked round his pack, sniffing the night air. 'I don't see Victor?'

The young wolves snickered amongst themselves, nose-pushing and play-biting until one said, 'Think he's collecting leaves and bilberries for his supper.'

Another said, 'When *we* were out savaging sheep. Yay!'

'That does it! No son of mine eats that rubbish when there's good, fresh meat to be had,' and he padded into the den on hard, purposeful paws.

Later when the snarling had finished and it was quict, Victor's mother was giving her youngest son a good talking to. 'Darling, I know you're not like the others, but at least eat some lamb heart along with the leaves, just for me?'

Inside the den, Victor wrinkled his beautiful aquiline nose, moved his paws delicately among the detritus of bones, rotting flesh and a small squirming thing being played with by the very youngest cub and knew that it was time to go.

*

He was sad to leave his family, but most of all, his mother, who'd shielded him. He knew he wasn't like his brothers. Now, tired and exhausted, he came at last to a cottage deep in the forest. Sinking down, he placed his muzzle on his front paws, and fell asleep.

'Oh my Gawd, what have we here?' Granny towered over him in patent leather high heels. 'I need to escape before my bossy little granddaughter Marigold gets here, but I can't leave you like this. Come on in.' She shooed him into the cottage. 'Looks as though you could do with a kip, my sweetheart,' Granny said. 'Just pop into bed – you can wear me pure satin nightgown to be comfy – look lovely against your fur.'

'What about your granddaughter – won't she be frightened, to see a wolf in bed instead of Granny? I mean, it looks really inviting, but I wouldn't want...'

'Don't you fret about that, son,' Granny said decisively, 'time I got me own back for all those sodding banana loaves she keeps bringing me.'

'Sounds delicious,' Victor said politely, and promptly fell asleep till morning.

*

The sound of heavy boots clomping into the cottage woke Victor from deep sleep. The slip and slither of satin sliding across his legs had given him the sweetest of dreams, and he was not as prepared as he should have been for the inquisition which now assaulted him. A girl with spiky black hair and a red cloak was leaning over the bed staring at him in an unfriendly manner.

'Hey Gran – what's with the eyes? They're a sort of funny green.'

'My dear, not quite so close, your breath's a little ripe, garlic I think?'

‘And your nose has gone all pointy and sharp.’

‘You’re very personal, I must have a word with your mother.’

‘And oh boy those gnashers! Are you using Brillo pads or what? They’re so cool!’

‘Thankfully you’ve just redeemed yourself in time,’ said Wolf, although he’d no intention of eating this obnoxious little girl, as he didn’t want to get blood on his lovely new nightgown. After they’d eaten the banana loaf, which Victor found greatly to his liking, he and Marigold had a long talk.

‘Gran won’t be back for ages once she’s in town, so stay round awhile. I so dig your fur,’ Marigold said, stroking the smooth pelt which varied in colour from almost pure white through shades of blond, cream and ochre.

‘And you can do as much of that as you like, young lady.’ Victor was changing his mind about Marigold, who seemed to have far better taste than he’d credited her with. Further searches in the food cupboard revealed 24 more banana bread loaves in varying stages of putrefaction, so Victor sent Marigold out into the forest to gather crab-apples, mushrooms and any other tasty berries she could find. Later, he changed into a red silk negligee with lace trimming, and a rather convenient pair of black French knickers, and they lolled in front of the cottage fire swapping life histories and playing cards. ‘Won’t your mother worry where you are?’ asked Victor. He imagined a search party who may not be as amenable to his presence.

‘Nah, think I’ve been eaten by a wolf, and only too glad to see the back of me. She’s in with a load of bossy women called Christabel, Emmeline and Sylvia. Spend their time arguing, being cross and making placards.'

*

Soft spring days passed. Victor taught Marigold Gin Rummy and Poker, Marigold trimmed and painted Victor's nails a beautiful vermilion red. They replaced Granny's dingy nets with swags of Laura Ashley. Little lambs nestled in front of the fire, wearing matching gingham bootees and suckling on warmed bottles of milk. 'Guilt is a terrible thing,' Victor admonished scornful Marigold as he wiped a droplet of milk from one of the lamb's noses. 'I have a great moral debt to all the sheep over the years whose clothing we wolves have borrowed.'

'Yeah, yeah, shut up and deal. You owe me too,' said Marigold.

Visitors came to the cottage lured by smells of simmering truffles in brandy and were offered delicious dishes of young sorrel leaves with cream washed down with crisp white wine. They returned, bringing friends, mistresses, lovers. A young woodcutter came by: 'He's got a big chopper,' Marigold said, and was cuffed by Victor who offered him a job as *Maitre d'* and bouncer. By then they'd turned Granny's spare room into one for 'overnight guests' – Victor would not tolerate *brothel*.

But much as he enjoyed it, Victor yearned for more. He moved to Paris, changed his name to *Virgine* and opened his Michelin star restaurant. You've probably heard of Virginia Wolf?

Regent's Park, 3am

Robert Billing

Have you wondered what they do,
At 3am, down at the zoo?
Do pandas pander to the chimps?
Do penguins gorge on rum-soaked shrimps?

Could alligators, and the crocs,
Sneak out and raid the shops for chocs?
Do adders, and those blind cave worms,
Play blackjack with the pachyderms?

While wildebeest and kangaroo,
Watch naughty films, eat popcorn too.
They might, because they know the joke
Is us. They call us window folk.

For we queue up, and even pay -
We do it almost every day,
So we can crowd around the glass,
While they lie flat out on the grass.

We mutter, 'Oh, you poor, tired thing'
At beasts worn out from partying.
But later, as the last gates close,
He's up, and wrinkling his nose.

Then dropping in the brown bear's cave,
For one quick pint, before the rave.
So think, before you quote *Born Free*,
No animal has ever paid to see,

What we do in our daily round.
But you – you parted with ten pound,
Then four more for that glossy book,
Before you've even had one look.

Thus giving up your hard-earned cash,
You're helping fund their nightly bash.
When leaning on the glass please think,
Of weasels that you've turned to drink,

And emus who have learned to smoke.
A camel once began to choke,
On pills he'd bought from a gazelle,
We saved him, but he's still not well.

But where can recovery begin,
For wildlife that's been brought down by gin?
Give us coins, and five pound notes,
To help with drying out the goats.

Inspired by playing Simon and Garfunkel's 'At The Zoo' and 'Wednesday Morning, 3am' back to back several times.

The Walking Tree

John Shepherd

A scar on my left shin is a permanent reminder of my visit to the rainforest in spring 2013.

'Oh, that's just an otter,' the guide remarked when I asked about the sleek dark animal crossing the meadow below. I'd never seen an otter in the wild before, but I suppose when you've recently seen three types of monkey, two types of sloth, racoons, dolphins, a silky anteater, several species of iguana, snake and lizard, and a walking tree, an otter is not so very exciting. Yes, I did say a walking tree. It might move at the pace that makes a snail look like a Formula One car, but because it lacks a tap root, if this tree fancies a move to a sunnier spot it will progressively grow more aerial roots in the desired direction and use these to pull the tree along. At least, that's what the guides told us.

With 25% of the country virgin rainforest, Costa Rica is rather like a game park with no boundary fence. Racoons and white headed capuchin monkeys could be seen from the hotel. Hummingbirds drank nectar from the flowers by our window. Colourful birds whose names we never learnt were everywhere. A lizard, known locally as the Jesus Christ lizard, entertained us by running across the hotel swimming pool.

Costa Rica is supposed to be noted for bananas, pineapple and coffee, but, where we were, neat rows of palm oil trees dominated the landscape. The trees were never allowed to get more than about 20 feet high because beyond that height, harvesting, which was done by hand, became uneconomical and the trees were then felled and a new crop planted. The plantations were manned largely by Nicaraguan immigrants; the locals not wanting to risk the aggressive fer-de-lance snakes which made their homes there.

Located between Nicaragua and Panama in Central America, Costa Rica isn't the easiest location to reach from the United Kingdom. We flew there via Canada, but a cheaper and shorter alternative might be found via Spain. Spanish is the national language although English is widely understood. Though the currency is the Costa Rican colón, we found that most hotels and many shops and tourist attractions accepted United States dollars.

And while Costa Rica may be poor by western standards, no way could it be called a backward country. It abolished its armed forces in 1949 and redirected the money into education. Depending on which figures you use, it has one of the highest literacy rates in the world and has also been ranked first in the Happy Planet Index. Its citizens enjoy a longer life expectancy than those of the United States.

While you don't need to visit a game park to see wildlife, it was in the Manuel Antonio National Park that I saw the two types of sloth and the howler and squirrel monkeys. The cacophonous cries of the howler monkeys alerted us to their presence long before we actually saw them. But you are almost guaranteed to see wildlife anywhere. The most imposing predator is the jaguar but they are secretive and nocturnal and your chances of seeing one almost zero.

While Costa Rica's climate is tropical all year long, if you want to minimise the prospect of rain, January to March is the best time to visit. The beaches and sea are warm and sandy, but we were warned to beware of savage rip currents.

'If you get caught in one, don't fight it,' I was told. 'Swim parallel to the shore and you should soon be free to swim back to land.' This information is probably sound, though I made sure that I was never in a position to test it. However, from personal experience I can pass on the following advice. Don't leave clothes unattended on the beach or they will be rifled through by racoons and monkeys.

A highlight of my trip was white water rafting down the Naranjo River. I had been rafting before in Scotland and was surprised that this trip started in a gently sloping rocky waterfall. I had expected an easier introduction. I soon realised my error. This was the easy stretch. For two hours we fended the rafts off rocks with our paddles while crashing down waterfall after waterfall. The paddles were seldom needed to propel us along. The river did that. It was the ultimate adrenaline trip. As we sped through virgin jungle, we had little time to observe the wildlife. However, one animal that we did see added spice to the occasion. A crocodile! I would like to say that I got my scar fighting off the crocodile but the truth is more mundane. I fell down the steps to the toilet.

Sunlight Training

Julie Roberts

Wilf shuffled for a space in the coal miners' lift. This was his last ride up. Never again would he taste the coal dust or joke with his mates deep in the bowels of the earth.

The government had won. He was redundant – too old to retrain. But how long would the pay off last? How long before he'd have to ask for social benefits? Could he face that? No. He would sooner jump back down the shaft than face that humiliation.

When Wilf reached his two-up, two-down mid-terrace house, he stood outside, reluctant to go in. Shame stood alongside his anger. He'd been bottling up his feelings for the past two weeks, since he'd opened the letter passed to him by the pit manager.

The house was empty; it always was when he was on the early shift. God, how was he going to face the pitying glances from the other men's wives? He put the key in the lock and went in. He would go straight to bed, then there was no chance of seeing anyone until tomorrow. It would give him a few hours to adjust. Adjust! Who was he kidding?

Wilf didn't sleep. He lay there thinking about the pit and about money, listening to the tick of the alarm clock. At last the shrill ring sounded, four o'clock, time to get up. But it wasn't necessary and it wouldn't be now until the day he died.

The sound of footsteps on the stairs told him his daughter, Molly, was going to make the tea. She knew there was no reason to get up so early now, it was just habit.

He pushed back the covers; *I can't stay in bed another minute.* It was a luxury he had never known and he didn't intend to start now. His feet touched the rag rug and he stood up and turned on the light. What was he going to wear? Not his miner's clothes. He opened the wardrobe door – there was his dark suit for funerals, his sports jacket and grey trousers he wore when he went to the Tattersley Miners' Club. It would have to be the greys. He opened the chest of drawers and took out a white shirt, socks, vest and pants and laid them on the bed.

When his Hilda died, Molly, who had recently been widowed, gave up her rented house and moved in with him. The only awkward thing about it was that he had always washed downstairs. Standing half-dressed at the scullery sink, with Molly around, was a tad embarrassing. So he'd decided to get a plumber to put a wash basin in his room and then life carried on much the same.

Now he filled that basin with hot water, lathered his face and shaved. Washed his face and neck and dried with a coarse towel. He took his false teeth from a glass of diluted bleach and rinsed them with cold water.

It was strange slipping his arms into a cotton shirt, instead of the dark flannel. He tucked the tails inside his trousers and buttoned the fly, then picked up a shoehorn to help his feet into his best shoes. He always polished them to a brilliant shine after every outing, so at least he had one job to do every day now.

As he passed the mirror on the wardrobe door it reflected a sight never allowed in the bedroom – his dull black work boots. He felt choked, almost bereaved, for his life now gone. He wiped his eyes with his knuckles.

It was time to go and face Molly.

'Good morning, Dad. We're a pair of dafties, getting up at this hour. We could both have had a lay-in. Still, I've made the tea. Sit down.'

Wilf sat in his usual chair, but he felt uncomfortable. What could he say to Molly? They usually only grunted at each other – he would have drunk his tea, picked up his sandwiches and left.

'Thanks.' He looked round the room. It hadn't changed much since he'd carried Hilda over the threshold forty years ago. This was where they lived – he called it the kitchen, Molly called it the living room. There was the mahogany table and four chairs, sideboard and two stuffed green armchairs. The only additions to mark the twentieth century were a stereo radio and a colour telly. He had felt that Molly deserved some modern pleasures when she moved in.

'Do you want any breakfast, Dad?'

Wilf looked at her and smiled. 'Why not? I've plenty of time now.'

'Bacon and egg?'

'It's not Sunday, Molly. I don't know. What are you going to have?'

'Oh, I just have toast and Marmite.'

'Then I'll have the same.'

Molly went out into the scullery. Wilf heard her strike a match and then the rattle of the enamel grill tray.

It was only five o'clock. What was he going to do all day?

Molly called, 'Dad, if you have time, there's a bit of veg left in the shed. Can you get it, I want to make a stew.'

Wilf didn't answer.

'Dad – did you hear me?'

'Yes. I suppose so. When do you want them?'

'By half-past seven. They have to simmer for several hours so we can have dinner at one o'clock.'

This was a new world for Wilf. Doing shift work had meant he ate either before or after a shift. Now he could have three meals a day sitting with Molly. What were they going to talk about? She didn't want to hear about the coal face or smirking men laughing at tales that weren't fit for women's ears.

'Right then, straight after the toast.'

Molly came back and put two plates on the table and sat down.

'Gwen at the corner shop is on holiday this week. I said I would help out. I have to be there at eight. Will you be all right?'

Wilf felt like a small boy. How had he gone from a miner, who risked life and limb year after year, to a dependant who couldn't be left for a few hours?

'I think, Molly, I can manage not to fall over or hurt myself. I've been doing it ever since I went to work nearly fifty years ago. Don't start fussing now.'

Molly sighed. 'Sorry, Dad, but … well, this is all new to you … I mean, having nothing to do.'

Nothing to do!

Wilf let these three words roll round in his mind. They horrified him. 'I'll go and get the veg. You get yourself ready. I'll be fine.'

The sun was climbing over the housetops that backed on to his row. Normally, he would only have had this fresh air walking to the pithead. He breathed in. The air felt cold slipping down his throat, stinging with pinpoint jabs. He closed his lips tight, then opened and breathed in again. This time he knew what to expect and enjoyed the sensation. He did it several times more. He would remember this as the first new experience of his retirement.

'Dad, can I have the veg, time's getting on.'

Wilf waved, 'Coming.'

After Molly left the house it was very quiet.

Sitting in his chair, the one to the left of the fireplace, he pondered whether to turn on the telly. Morning programmes were for the women or schools. But what else was there to do? Hilda had kept house and he'd earned the money. It was as it should be, as his father and his before him had done.

Wilf turned the television on and a newsreader filled the screen. He tuned to another channel – an advert for grass fertiliser, demanding that the viewer tend their gardens with weekly nourishment as spring was round the corner. The screen flicked to Stork margarine – two young women trying to tell the difference from butter. He turned it off.

They didn't have much grass, just a small patch to sit on in the back. It always looked weedy and those wretched daisies and clover made up most of it anyway. Perhaps, as he had time now, he could make an effort to give Molly something nice to sit on. Do a few flowers in a border. He had always grown veg – Hilda had insisted, said they tasted better than those from Greenfingers in the High Street.

After a cup of chicory flavoured coffee, Wilf thought about the grass again. It would be a token of his appreciation, Molly never asked him to do much, just the jobs she couldn't manage.

Ten minutes later, Wilf locked the front door and set off for the local garden nursery. He reckoned it was about a two mile walk – another first for him – his usual distance was the half mile to the club for a pint or the same to the pit.

He was out of breath by the time he arrived at Snelgrove Nurseries. It was surrounded by a privet hedge with a wooden gate anchored open. In the centre was an oversized shed with a sign saying: *Everything you want for your garden – Come on in.* That sounded like a good invitation, so he did just that.

'Good morning, sir. If there's anything you can't see, just ask. I'm Charlie.'

Wilf looked at the shelves – bottles, cans and plastic containers stood like soldiers in rows. Watering cans, netting and plant pots covered the floor, leaving barely enough room for him to walk round.

'I'm looking for grass fertiliser,' said Wilf, twisting his neck to try and locate what he wanted.

'Third shelf on the left, behind you.'

'Thanks.'

'You new to the area?'

Wilf wanted to laugh at that. 'No. I've lived all my life in Tattersley.'

'Just retired, then?'

'Well … yes, I suppose I am.'

Wilf's life crowded in on him. No, he wasn't retired, he was unwanted. There were years left in him to work the pit, but they'd said no. *Be a good man and take the money – sit back and enjoy retirement.* He didn't want retirement – he wanted to work.

Suddenly the shop seemed to shrink and close in on him. 'I'll just go and have a look outside – be back in a minute.'

Wilf wasn't really interested; it was just an excuse to get away from the man. But as he walked, he noticed the shrubs and plants along the paths. They added colour amongst the green leaves – new life struggling to grow – waiting for those keen gardeners to pluck them from the trays and set them into the earth, waiting for gentle rain and warm sun to make them blossom. These thoughts chased away Wilf's dark moment and he wandered amongst the foliage, enjoying it far more than he would have ever thought.

After much deliberation, Wilf took a tray of polyanthus, four rose bushes – one of each colour – and pansies back into the shop.

'That's a good start for the season, sir. Did you want the grass feed?'

'Yes, please.'

The man came round from the counter. He limped, much the same as Wilf did when his knee ached.

'A touch of arthritis, I'm afraid. Standing a lot plays it up.'

'That makes two of us. Got mine down the black hole.'

'This isn't a large nursery to run, but I think Old Father Time is trying to tell me something. I've run this place for ten years single-handed, since my Doris passed away, but I think now's the time to seek a little help.'

Wilf nodded, understanding that both of them were suffering, but in different ways.

'I didn't want to give up either. The pit was my world, my life, like gardening is yours. Ageing can be a bum of a cross to bear. This is my first day of *retirement.* They think they are doing me a favour, but they're not. I *want* to work.'

The man nodded. 'A bum cross to bear,' and tapped in the prices of Wilf's goods.

'Cheque or cash?'

'Cash. Is taking cheques a good idea?'

'Latest thing now. The white collar workers are all being paid that way.'

'Oh.' There didn't seem anything else to say.

Wilf parted with his money and realised he wasn't going to be able to carry it all home.

'Stupid me. I can't carry that lot two miles. I'll have to come back this afternoon for some of it.'

'You don't have a car then?'

'No. Never had a use for one – shift work doesn't lend itself to gallivanting about.'

'Sorry, I don't deliver. Although ... what if I come after closing time?'

'It would be a help. Sure you don't mind?'

'Take what you want for today and I'll see you later with the rest.'

Wilf showed his gratitude with a smile. '46 Wheelers Terrace, half way along on the left.'

He picked up the box of grass fertiliser tucked it under his arm and waved goodbye.

*

At six o'clock, Wilf heard a knock on the front door.

The garden man stood with the tray of pansies in his hand. 'As promised, all goods delivered as ordered.'

'Come in. We'll take them straight through to the back.'

Molly was filling the kettle when both men came into the kitchen 'What's all this about, Dad?'

'This is Charlie, from the garden nursery. He's delivered the goods I bought this morning. It's for a little gardening job I have in mind. Charlie, this is my daughter, Molly.'

'Nice to meet you, Molly.'

'And you, Charlie. This is kind of you.'

'Cuppa when we've finished?'

'Five minutes, Dad, and it'll be ready.'

Wilf put the rose bushes down by the shed. 'Here will do for now. Thanks for bringing them.'

'Glad to help.'

Wilf held his arm out, indicating the wooden bench. 'It's still pleasant, shall we have our tea here. I'm Wilf by the way.'

They sat quietly, looking at the garden.

'A fair size plot,' Charlie commented. 'I see you grow your own veg, and this is a pleasant bit of grass to rest your feet on. South facing too, but not enough to keep you busy all day.'

'No.'

The man's remark dug deep, emphasising the grudge that lodged like a stone in his belly.

‘I’ve been thinking this afternoon about my business. If I had someone to help out, I could advertise a delivery service. What would you say to a part-time job?’

Wilf didn’t answer.

‘Sorry, I shouldn’t have jumped in like a bull in a china shop.’

‘No. You just took me by surprise. A part-time job? But I’m no expert on gardening. True, I have always turned my hand to this bit, but help with your lot…’

‘What you do here is no different, not really, mine’s just bigger. Whether you grow one carrot or a hundred, the way you do it is the same. I could give you some training. Especially on the bits you might be dodgy with.’

Wilf couldn’t think clearly. ‘I don’t know. Training you say? Like, teaching me the ropes?’

‘Yes, and at the going rate per hour.’

‘I don’t want a charity handout.’ Wilf’s voice had a bitter note to it.

The man ran his fingers through his sparse grey hair. ‘Look, Wilf, there’s no charity here; a good day’s work for a fair day’s pay. You help me and I can help you.’

Wilf sat quietly and thought for a moment about the man’s offer. He had worked hard in the darkness of the pit to earn his bread. This was a chance to work in the sunlight to keep that bread on the table. He could breathe in the fresh air each day, as he had this morning. Cleanse his lungs of the black dust. He would be out of Molly’s way, give the house to her like she was used to. He could look his mates in the eye when he went to the club for a drink. Buy his round, as he always had.

He was worth training?

Wilf smiled, thinking of that upstart in the pit office.

Straightening up, he squared his shoulders. 'I'll give it a go, Charlie. Thanks for the offer.'

Charlie held out his hand. 'Done. See you tomorrow at nine o'clock.'

As promised, Molly came through the kitchen door carrying a tray. 'Tea's up, boys.'

'Oh, I think we can do better than that,' laughed Wilf. 'Bring out that whisky left from Christmas. I've got a new job to celebrate. Charlie's going to train me up to be a garden salesman!'

The Root of All Evil

Based on 'The Pardoner's Tale' by Geoffrey Chaucer

J. E. Cohen

Steven, you don't know how glad I am to see you. I've had a horrible week, all this media frenzy about that guy in Tennessee. My phone's been ringing nonstop. It's ridiculous. This psycho in Tennessee picks up a chainsaw and ploughs a bloody path through his local McDonald's and they're blaming it on my *movie*? Have you ever heard anything so stupid?

And today I've got the lawyers from the studio on the phone, saying that we're gonna get sued by the dead people's families, and by the family of this guy who did it, and by the makers of the damn chainsaw, even by McDonald's for God's sake, just because our movie supposedly gave this guy the idea. I mean for one thing, the killer in *Chainsaw Frenzy* doesn't kill people in a McDonald's. He kills them in a Burger King. Also, this Tennessee guy was a real psycho. He tortured cats and stuff. He didn't need *Chainsaw Frenzy* to make him into a weirdo.

Okay, he was obsessed with the movie, apparently had four copies of it on DVD, but it's a free country. Nobody *made* him buy a chainsaw and start dismembering people. My *movie* certainly didn't. Three million people saw that movie in its first week alone and how many of them went right out and bought a chainsaw?

Exactly.

Yeah, I'll have a dirty martini, thanks.

People are such hypocrites. Movies are the major moral force in this country today. People aren't going to church, they don't trust the government, there are liars and cheats all over the newspapers and you know why people go watch a movie? Because the movies are one of the last places in the world where the bad guys get punished. People are crucifying me because I made *Chainsaw Frenzy* and *Death World* and *Blood Feast* and I'm glamorising violence, yadda, yadda, yadda, but in every single one of those films the killer gets it in the end in a horrific way. That's what sends them out smiling, all the way to the mall to buy the T-shirt and the action figures.

Hold on, I've gotta take this call, it's the wife.

Hello? Yeah, Celine, I'm busy. Listen, sweetheart, I won't be home 'til late tonight. I've got a meeting. No, don't wait up. Okay, baby, see you tomorrow. Bye.

Celine believes everything I tell her. I don't have a meeting, I'm seeing this girl I auditioned for *Death World*. She can't act, but she has a lot of other talents.

Like I was saying, we're practically the guardians of the nation's soul, you and me.

Speaking of which, you are gonna love this project I've got for you. It's practically a Bible story, it's so damn holy. Let me order another martini and I'll tell you.

It starts out with these three narcotics cops. Buddies. About to make a bust at an abandoned warehouse. This bust is so huge, it's so secret, that they haven't told their superiors about it. They're gonna catch the gang red-handed, bring in the cash and the drugs, and get some serious promotion.

Their lives aren't so great. One guy, I think we should get Ray Liotta, his wife's about to leave him because he's been sleeping around and he hits her when he's stressed. And the second, I'm thinking Jason Statham, he's about to lose everything because he's got this secret gambling problem. And the third guy, he's this Samuel L. Jackson badass type, he's got a serious heroin monkey.

They get to the warehouse just as the deal's going down and they're about to jump in and arrest everyone when suddenly the guys who are buying the drugs turn on the other guys and waste them all. Our cops are watching this, they're trying to stay cool, but Jackson, he hasn't had a fix in a while, he makes a noise. There's this really tense standoff and then Liotta's temper takes over and he starts shooting. Then it all kicks off, bullets flying, the floor of the warehouse is littered with corpses, arms shot off, heads exploding, everything.

Fantastic.

So all the scumbags are dead and here's our three cops, standing in a blood-soaked warehouse and they open this big crate in the middle of the carnage and it's full of drugs.

And all the people who knew about it are dead, and nobody on the force knows about it but them, and they've all got major problems that could be solved with an enormous chunk of cash. Which is also there, in a briefcase that's still handcuffed to one of the dead guys. You can imagine what they have to do to get it off him.

So they decide to keep it all – sell the drugs, keep the cash, disappear to South America. Liotta's dreaming about pricey whores, Statham's got his mind on casinos and Jackson's already jacking up some of the heroin. The thing is, they need to get it away from these dead bodies, and they know it's not safe to move the stuff until it gets dark.

Yeah, I'll have another drink, thanks. Okay, this is where it starts getting interesting. They're waiting around, so they send the wife-beater to get some food, McDonald's or wherever – no, hold on, I'm not touching McDonald's after what their lawyer said about *Chainsaw Frenzy* this morning. Liotta'll go to Krispy Kreme.

While he's gone, the junkie turns to the gambler and says, 'You know we'd get more money if we only had to split it two ways.' He convinces the gambler to shoot the wife-beater when he gets back. Of course, we know, from the glint in the junkie's eyes, that he's planning to get rid of the gambler as soon as he can, because there's going to be twice as much money if he doesn't have to split it at all.

Meanwhile, the wife-beater is adding it up himself. He visits one of his underworld contacts, who gets him this deadly poison. He puts it in two of the coffees, and goes back to the warehouse.

So the gambler shoots him, and after he's done the deed, the other two sit down for some donuts and coffee, and man, this poison is nasty. The special effects we could do on that one, I'm thinking we'd surpass even *Blood Feast.*

Fantastic, right? And get this – it's so moral even the God Squad will love it. Greed, violence, drugs, adultery, gambling, it all gets punished in the end. And the title, listen to this: *The Root of All Evil.* This one is gonna rake it in, Steven. You think Samuel L. will say yes?

Hey, listen, I've gotta run. What with dodging phone calls and getting updates from my lawyer every hour I'm practically ready to go on a chainsaw rampage myself. If it weren't for the coke I'd've collapsed by now.

Thinking about it, of course I'm sorry for all those people who died in McDonald's, but it could be a blessing in disguise. The only bad publicity's no publicity, right? You know how much income cult films can make?

That guy in Tennessee might have done us a favour.

COMING HOME

Kalkan

Claire Dyer

'The place nearest to the stars', *Herodotus*

And it's how the olive trees don't speak,
but are wise with wisdoms anyway,
wisdoms that are words in the wind

from the mountains, trout farms of Islamlar,
the ice streams and the road to Fethiye
and the sun is a blood orange in the sky;

how the grasses, silver jut of rocks
have something of music,
of the *muezzin's* daily call in them;

how a cat came to the gate today
and feral-stared at me with her one blue,
one green eye and opened her mouth,

how her kittens called for her
and she disappeared in the *zeytinlik*,
a flash of white like snow –

I could tell she was pregnant again.
The *gulets* are returning now,
leaving shapes like arrowheads in the water

and later the moon will rise,
drop its light magnificent in the harbour.
The stars are closest here to anywhere on earth.

In the Old Town will be candlelight,
waiters cracking open Pitcher Kebabs.
Spiced steam will rise; will catch the back

of my throat for you
not knowing this,
for the already gone of it.

Note: muezzin – person appointed at a mosque to lead, and recite the call to prayer; zeytinlik – olive garden; gulet – two or three-masted wooden sailing vessel.

The Village of Visions

Charles Whittaker

Charles lived and worked for several years in Portugal, and has maintained close links with that country, especially with the small village which forms both the setting and the central character of this piece.

Once upon a time, in an age of religion and chivalry, a nobleman, Dom Fuas Roupinho, travelled from his castle in the hills at Porto de Mos to the coast. It took two days to reach his favourite hunting grounds – the pine forests that grew alongside the silvery beaches and the Atlantic Ocean. On the second morning, a thick fog crawled in from the sea and settled across the land. Dom Fuas saw the shape of a stag in the gloom. He set off in chase, ordering his entourage to follow. His companions were slow and lost him in the mist. A keen huntsman, he rode on, alone. Glimpsing the ghostly outline of the deer among the trees, he spurred his horse onwards in pursuit.

He soon found himself close to the sea. He could hear the distant rumbling of waves against rocks, smell salt and seaweed on the breeze. He heard, too, the sound of the fleeing deer ahead. Suddenly there was a bright light in the sky, the mist cleared and there, among the clouds, was a vision of Our Lady, the mother of Christ, warning him to stop. His horse reared at the sight, its hooves biting into the hard rocks at the very edge of a high cliff rising dramatically above the sea. The vision came too late for the stag, which ran out into the air and fell. A deeply religious man, Dom Fuas knew he had seen a miracle. He dismounted and fell to his knees giving thanks to God and to the Virgin Mary for his deliverance.

Dom Fuas recognised the barren promontory where he knelt. Below in a grotto, guarded by a hermit, lay a small wooden statue of Mary with the child Jesus on her knee. It had been brought from Jerusalem to Spain and then, in 711AD, to Portugal by a friar, Romano, and the defeated King Rodrigo fleeing the invading Moors. The carving was said to have been made by Saint Joseph himself when Jesus was a small child. In gratitude, the nobleman had a tiny chapel built on the cliff edge above the cave. They decorated the roof with a pyramid of hand-painted tiles, blue, white and yellow, to protect it from the rain. Inside, too, tiles covered the walls and ceiling, depicting religious scenes of saints and martyrs. He dedicated it to Nossa Senhora da Nazareth, where the statue had been carved.

The bare uninhabited headland was known only as Sitio da Nazareth, the site of Nazareth. Word of the miracle spread in those religious times, bringing pilgrims. Across centuries kings, too, came to this desolate place. To house the statue they built a bigger church in an elegant square, added cloisters, domes, bell towers and even a hospital.

Four hundred years later, in a world of commerce and discovery, a man with a different vision stood on that same promontory, a handsome 37 year-old with a full beard beneath a long nose and dark piercing eyes. He looked down on his ship, the *São Gabriel,* below in the sandy bay, sheltered from the prevailing wind that would take him south to Lisbon and a place in history ... if he survived.

Vasco da Gama, third son of a knight of the Order of Santiago, foresaw a journey around Africa to the lands of the east, never before reached from Europe by sea. He would be the first, bringing wealth to his country and to his king, João II, Master of the Order. God still occupied men's minds and Vasco naturally sought His blessing. The most venerated site of pilgrimage in all of Portugal was none other than the tiny chapel of Dom Fuas. Inside, he gazed at the tiles. Tiny religious figures, blue on white, stared back at him as he fell to his knees. He prayed for an hour or more, his rosary clicking rapidly through his fingers, praying for protection against the perils he was to face. Many before him had died in the attempt. Finally, he stood and made his way down the cliff to the beach below.

After an absence of more than two years, Vasco returned to Nazaré to give thanks for his successful voyage. Fame and fortune followed. Given the title of *Dom*, he made two more voyages to India before being appointed as Viceroy and Governor of Portuguese India. How much of this future he saw in this vision is not known, but thousands of visitors come in buses and cars each year to see the place where he stood, the chapel where he prayed and the church built by kings. These new pilgrims rarely attend Mass or even stop to pray, preferring rather to worship the sun.

The bay below adopted the name Nazareth, since corrupted to Nazaré, and became a thriving fishing village where craggy-faced men in small craft rowed out to catch cod in the North Atlantic. Many died in the attempt. Their wives wore short skirts so they could help haul the fish-laden boats up on to the long beach that Vasco and Dom Fuas had seen. Their short skirts with seven layers were a triumph of practicality over centuries of religious prudery. When not hauling in boats, they wore thick woollen socks and shawls to stay warm in the cold winters and the piercing winds from the north. Today, older women still wear the seven skirts as they sell woollens, pottery or dried fish and fruit to the tourists; the young wear jeans.

In a new century a new pilgrim comes, a man named Garrett McNamara. Not by horse or on foot, not even by car or bus, he flies his private jet half-way across the world from his home in Hawaii. He too has a vision – to surf the tallest wave in the world, for it will bring him fame and fortune. Unbeknown to Dom Fuas or Vasco da Gama, outside the headland of Sitio da Nazaré, God had placed an underwater canyon, over two kilometres deep. Caribbean storms cross the Atlantic, pilgrim-like, for days, before funnelling up the canyon. As it narrows towards the shore and the sea rises up, as if in gigantic imitation of Dom Fuas' horse, higher even than the lighthouse that now stands on the end of the promontory. A jet ski, like a buzzing insect scuttling across the swell, tows the American to the top of the wave where foam curls above him as he hurtles down the glistening blue wall into the record books and history. Thousands of pilgrims come in awe to see this taming of Nature. Millions watch on YouTube.

Shirl's Girls

Juliet England

'I'm Beverley. I'm quite strange.'

Having arrived before me, Beverley has already hit the beach. She is in her sixties with pale, frizzy hair.

Still disoriented by the journey and a night on the (carpet) tiles in Gatwick's North Terminal, I am nonplussed by her introduction – she doesn't seem the slightest bit strange to me.

This is Lefkas. This is Nikiana, on its eastern coast road. And this is Serenity Retreat. More women, their pastiness betraying their Britishness, emerge from the apartment buildings fronting onto the pebbled beach. At the taverna round the corner, we hear each other's stories over Greek salad and chips. The Holy Grail of 'gelling' is instantaneous. These are (in every sense of the word) big women, real women, women who life has taken in its jaws and tossed around. There is none of that 'Where have you come from?' awkwardness I've encountered on other group holidays.

That night, I sleep oblivious to the newness of the apartment. (Apartment is, in truth, something of an exaggeration. The place is really a bedroom with a stove, small bathroom and tiny balcony. But I love its view over rooftops, washing lines, flower baskets, and the glittering prize of the Ionian Sea, the light dancing on it like paparazzi flashbulbs.)

I wake before seven and take tea to the shore before the heat and light have got down to business.

Heather is also up, but stays on the veranda. We both know, instinctively, that sometimes conversation has no place.

At lunch, there are more introductions – to bewitching Miriam from Northern Ireland, a chain smoker with a laugh as rough as sandpaper, and Carolyn from LA whose headphones are a constant umbilical cord to her iPad, as she speaks ceaselessly to her boyfriend in America.

'John?' she drawls. 'Jaaaahn?'

We all refuse to believe she's 52.

Pat, a counsellor from London, lets the tears roll down her cheeks as she speaks. This is her first holiday after the death of her husband of two decades.

Ballsy Kim, who runs the show, has been mauled around by life more than most. Without a shred of self-pity, she explains she is a former alcoholic who tried to kill herself three times. Jill is here to avoid her ex-husband, who is remarrying that week.

We call ourselves Shirl's Girls, as in Shirley Valentine. The cliché of a bunch of middle-aged women descending in Greece, alone but for each other, does not escape us. What are we looking for? Romance? We don't find it, with each other or anyone else, and Tom Conti is nowhere to be seen.

To help with the quest, a 'Heal Your Life' course is being run all week, although I can't understand why these sassy, brilliant women would feel any need to heal their lives. When I ask how it went each day, they always reply with the same words: 'Lots of tears'.

I have a crack at a meditation session but am quickly distracted by a buzzing fly. It's not for me.

I fare better with an early morning stroll into the hills, giving ridiculously beautiful views over the island, herby smells, the clang of goat bells and every other Greek cliché going. Jane, leading the hike, makes us walk partly in silence, the better to absorb everything. It works.

While the girls heal their lives, I go off exploring by bus. Unlike its brassier cousin Nidri up the road, Nikiana is untouristy, but the pebble beach is its only real attraction.

I make for Vassiliki, in the island's deep south, and take a boat to Agiofilli, one of the most perfect beaches I have ever seen. Burning white sand, glassy turquoise water over rocks slimy with moss. A beach backed by sheer white cliffs.

The villages inland are also worth exploring. In Karya I love the huge plane trees in the ancient main square, the almost perpendicular streets and the eccentric lace museum. Here life has repelled the tourist invasion, carrying on almost unchanged at its glacial pace forever.

In the evenings, the other Shirl's Girls and I meet by the low, sun-warmed stone wall outside the apartments to go for dinner, locally or in Lefkas town, at the gorgeous main square. Walking back, I stop to stare at the butterball moon flooding the sea's still surface.

There is a tacky, hilarious Greek Night, at which balancing a table on your head is obligatory and the star of the show is 'Mama', well into her eighties and a walking, gurning ad for the Olivio-based Mediterranean lifestyle.

Another evening we pile onto a beach on the mainland and lie looking up at the constellations as Steve 'unwraps the stars' mysteries'. The whole thing is not as magical as it sounds – Steve is a bit of an old ham and, in the dark, I can barely hear what he is saying.

The best, though, is saved for last when five of us take a boat out. 'Captain Bev' rashly agrees to let me take the tiller. Inevitably, I nearly steer us into the path of oncoming vessels. I feel a horrible urge to skinny dip, like Shirley did, although somehow can't quite bring myself to suggest it.

But I have learnt something. To exist completely in the moment. To focus on the feel of the water as I trail my wrist in it. To hear the engine's gentle purr and smell the oil fumes, suntan lotion and salt and feel the sun microwaving my skin. I let everything else fall away.

Next morning, as we say our goodbyes in the bar, I am surprised (and mildly embarrassed) to find myself brushing away tears, maybe because, deep down, I know I won't see these women again. We become Facebook friends, there is talk of meeting in Greece the following summer, of visiting Carolyn in LA, but, perhaps inevitably, it never happens. We were Shirl's Girls for one week only.

No. 83

Josh Williams

There's another world
where we're lovers
tender hateful lazy
lovers so busy
with each other

we don't recognise the stop.

But in this harsh light
you glance at me
as I push past
with eyes like winter
trapped in glass.

Do-It-Yourself

H. Piekarz

He was no longer forced to be pleasant to the customers. In ten days' time the lease on the shop ran out, and the automatic doors would be closed forever. James couldn't wait.

'No, that's all we've got left.' He wouldn't be reduced to apologising any more.

'Oh.' The clingy young couple dissolved back into the throng of trolleys. Disappointed, eh? I'll show you let down.

He checked the time on his till: 12:14. Not far until lunch. But he'd still have to keep up his energy to match the frenetic rate that these bargain hunters were streaming through the checkouts. He was tired from the morning, the repetitive left hand swung along the belt, tempered by the occasional stand up to scan a grow bag, or even better, planks of wood, when he'd leave his till and have to hunt for the bar code. That was about as far as he stretched his brain these days.

'Hi there, do you need a bag?' Was this what he had been reduced to? He didn't care. Ten more days and he'd be out of here. It was just a job; he'd find another. It was the people that he'd miss: super-sized Steve, grumpy Gary, the divine Barbara. Granted, another wouldn't be as close to home, or as mindlessly dumb as this one, but there'd be other jobs. His mind flashed to the rejection letter from the supermarket that he'd read over his cornflakes that morning. Still, the Royal Mail hadn't replied yet. People would always need letters.

He swore to himself that he wouldn't come begging to the Swedish flat-pack monopoly that were about to put him out of a job. They can stick their meatballs and über-warehouse with underground car park. As far as he was concerned, he wouldn't be setting foot in the new place. He remembered when they decided to build this HomeWares store, the years of council meetings and public planning hearings; all the locals kicked up a fuss about the loss of the green fields and the amount of traffic. It didn't have the disastrous impact that they were all worried about. Thrown a couple of horses out of their grazing field, that was all. It feels like this place has always been here, the tarmac sweep of the road had led to HomeWares for centuries, and not just to the Tudor manor at the top of the hill.

James remembered coming on the opening day, how the blue, shiny steel walls and clean, thick concrete made it look like an alien spaceship had landed in the field. Everyone was used to it now, the building was starting to look shabby in comparison to the spotless gaudy pink plastic of the computer store that had sprung up next door and the clear polished glass front of the carpet warehouse.

'Got any four by eights left, mate?'

'If we do, they'll be over behind the doors. Way over there.' He nodded in the direction. In days gone by, he'd automatically take them over to the shelf, and point out the selection on offer.

'Ta, mate.'

Chippy was just as happy to be nodded towards the route, and strode off in his plaster-splodged combats to find it himself.

A dark woman in a black beret stuck at a wonky angle was loitering nearby. As she approached him, he noticed she was wearing a pillar box red woollen coat and black leather gloves. He knew the score. Nothing in her hand but a carrier bag, a glance around for customer services, slight trepidation. 'Customer service disappeared when they all got laid off, madam.'

'I'm sorry, could I get a refund from you?' She pulled out a crinkled-up receipt from her pocket, and flattened it out over the counter.

James rolled his eyes towards the foil-covered pipework of the ventilation system. He exhaled a slow, deep sigh of damp cement air. He'd been doing this all morning long, and cursed the ignorance of the public.

'It states clearly on the front door, there's no returns or refunds. Right underneath "EVERYTHING MUST GO – ALL STOCK HALF MARKED PRICE".'

The lady wrinkled her forehead in an equal but opposite proportion to the amount that she'd just smoothed her raggedy receipt. She narrowed her eyes at him. 'But I'm within my consumer rights. I still have the statutory fourteen days to return an unwanted item.'

Damn these 'Watchdog' types. Anne Robinson has a lot to answer for.

'Right. So what's the problem with it?'

'It's no longer needed. My husband and I have–' she bit her lip, '–no use for this one-coat emulsion in "Candyfloss".' It's her turn to take a deep breath. 'Please.'

The old emotional routine still managed to soften him, and James scratched his temple. 'I'll see what I can do, eh?'

The ghost management weren't present on the shop floor anymore, so he made the decision. The refund option on the till hadn't been disabled, and he scanned the two tins through. Two quantity, five litres @ £18.49. Reason code – discontinued. Subtotal – £36.98. The till pinged open its gaping spring-loaded jaw, and James loaded the gloved hand up with cash. He smiled to reciprocate the one the lady had just given him. What's the worst they could do?

He checked the time on his till again. 12:31. Like a cuckoo clock, Syed appeared from the mirrored glass staff door behind the tills.

'All right, James. Off you go now. And enjoy.'

'Will do.' James logged out of his till and didn't need telling. He was up the stairs like a hungry man, pulling his stupid baseball cap from his head on the way. He entered the cramped staff room, which had the familiar odour of hot trainers and sweet 'n' sour soup-in-a-cup. Barbara was 31 minutes into her break and was sat snapping into an apple like a goddess. James took his Tupperware box from his locker, and mirrored her. Only ten more days. He'd have to do something pronto.

She swallowed her mouthful. 'All right, James.'

'Yes. Good day?'

'Not so bad.' She flicked through the pages of the free magazine that had been left on the table for days.

James peeled the lid off from his box, to reveal the ham sandwiches he'd neatly loaded there this morning. The butter had gone all squishy between the white slices. Just as he liked it.

'Still crazy down there?'

'Yeah, like the world's about to end. People, eh?' He mock tutted and nibbled on.

'I'll be glad to get out of here. The florist's is going to be like a breath of fresh air in comparison.' She pushed the magazine away.

'So you've found a new place?'

'Uh huh. Full time and no evenings.'

'Well done.' She's free every evening.

'Thanks. Any luck yourself?'

'Nope, still waiting to hear back from people.' She wants to know my prospects.

'Ah ha. They'll be knocking on your door soon enough.'

She has faith in me.

'Listen, Barbara, I was wondering, um…' She looked right at him. 'Mm … did you fancy a tea?'

She leant back in her chair and smiled. 'Thanks, James, that'd be lovely.' She checked her watch.

James flicked on the kettle and showed her all of his domestic prowess. 'Got to use up all these tea bags before they go to waste.'

He brought two mugs back to the table and they sipped in silence. The clock on the wall hit the hour and Barbara put her fleece back on and prepared to leave him.

'Catch you later, James.'

'Will do.' Nine more lunch breaks left.

He finished off his tea, accompanied by his chocolate sandwich biscuit, surgically peeled from its wrapper and dunked. It would be the last guaranteed moment of pleasure he would have until he arrived back at home. James savoured it, deep in his own private thoughts inside this windowless space. He smoothed his hair down, replaced his cap and checked his shirt front for crumbs.

He looked down at his name badge. 'Simon'. He was overjoyed when Simon took voluntary redundancy; his only redeeming feature was the use of his name badge when James left his own on the side of the washing machine. He tripped downstairs and returned to his post.

'Thanks, Syed. I'll do the returns for you, if you'd like.'

'Hey, no problem man.' Syed shrugged, in the middle of serving a customer.

James bent down to pick up the little basket of accumulated goodies that had been left at his till, and set off on his merry trail to put them back on the shelves. He wasn't quite ready to settle down for an afternoon of scanning and bagging just yet.

He wandered up the paint aisle, found the sickly shades of pink, and left two tins of "Candyfloss" someplace where he'd found a space on a mostly empty shelf. He moved onto the next item in his basket – grass seed. Up by the indoor gardening section, after the hosepipes. It was a fair walk away, but he found the gap on the shelf where it had been picked out from, and slid it back into the space.

'Sorry, mate, do you work here?' The bean pole frame of a man approached him. 'I'm looking for onion sets. Red, Ailsa Craigs.'

'Yeah, they should be just on the end here.' They walked in unison to the end. James shook his head at the state of the empty, grimy shelves. 'I think it's getting too late to be coming in here with a wish list.'

'Never mind, it was worth a try.'

James had found homes for all the items in his now swinging basket, and went to return to the tills, via the grand patio doors that marked the entrance to outdoor planting. He was hoping to catch a passing glimpse of Barbara out there. He lingered there, but couldn't see her. There were plenty of people outside, rummaging through shrubbery and poking at the pots. But none as beautiful as Barbara. He returned to the tills and settled himself in for an afternoon of daydreaming.

He kicked himself; all the time that he'd wasted here and not done anything about it.

'Do you have a reward card?'

They'd gone out to the local pub together, the company bash at Christmas. Had a bit of a boogie together afterwards, and then taken their separate buses home.

'Four seventy-eight.'

He racked his brains for a way of asking her.

Bing-bong: 'Would the customer asking about all-purpose grout please return to the information desk.'

The Tannoy always made you sound like you had a cold. He realised – that was it, the voice from the heavens had answered his prayer. He'd ask her as a public announcement. *Bing-bong:* 'Would Barbara from Outdoors please go out with James from checkouts.' Simple. Romantic.

'Hey, buddy, my change?'

'Oh, sorry, I was … here you go. Two pounds and a penny.'

James waited and waited for the last hour to come. The queues were a doddle to serve when you had something to look forward to. The store lights dimmed into dark recesses as the place bedded down for the night. At 18:45 James hit the wall, and the hungry-tiredness kicked in. He looked around for assistance. The customers had tapered away to stragglers now.

The clockwork vision of Syed appeared, and James called over to him as he approached the microphone.

'Syed, mind if I do it tonight?'

'No problem, mate.' He held his hands up, and walked back to the office.

James licked his lips, then gave a cough. He knew exactly the words he was going to say. He pushed the red button on his till, and leant right up close to the metal gauze of the speaker. He gulped.

'Ladies and gentlemen … er … the time is six fifty and the store will be closing in ten minutes. Could you make your way to the tills…?' His finger slipped from the red button, and he sank down into his seat.

He dispatched the last of the public, and couldn't wait to leave.

Bagged and coated, he pulled open the heavy fire door of the staff exit, to reveal a rainstorm. Just perfect, sums up the whole of my day.

He pulled his cagoule tight and ran across the car park. When he'd almost reached the break in the hedge to the footpath, he noticed a little car, and a lady fighting with an umbrella. He looked again, and it was Barbara, struggling with two bags of patio roses, and brolly, wrestling with her car keys.

He stepped in.

'Here, Barbara, let me.'

James picked the umbrella out from her hand, and held it aloft above the pair of them.

'Oh, James. Thank you.'

'I've been wandering for some time now, would you be free on an evening to go out with me, perhaps?'

Barbara looked up at him. 'I'd love to. I'm free in, oh, ten days' time?'

'Perfect.'

The rain pattered about them like applause, and Barbara tip-toed him a kiss on the cheek.

James glowed, confident that it was the beginning of growing their own home together.

We Used to Play

Alana James

Do you remember how we used to play?
Pat a cake, pat a cake,
chasing round the playground as fast as you can.
Hop, jump, skip and
Tag you're it.
Childhood games where the fallen could get up again

to grow older and play
drinking games.
Never Have I Ever been so drunk
as the time we played Fuzzy Ducks
in the Union.
They dared you to kiss me and

over the years we shared all our truths.
Piercing deep within
our skins, with wrists bound
by lust and sweat and musky scents.
Foreplay and bedroom games, where pleasure and pain co-existed
and no-one really resisted

until all our safe words were gone.
What remains are the words best left unsaid,
the shame and blame and
headfuck games which make it
hard to remember how
we used to play.

'We Used to Play' was written for the Reading Writers 2013 Spring Poetry Competition.

Magic and Water

R.J.F. Chalmers

'Magic is the curse of our world. We will never be rid of it, we will never control it, but I can teach a few of you to repel it. The only way to do this is with water, the water inside you. Water is life. Magic is death. And once death is upon you ... life can never overcome it. Come to understand this and you will live forever.'

I have spoken those words three times before. That may not sound like many, but when I start teaching a single class how to control death the task will not be complete for half a decade or more. It is no mean feat to repel death itself. I'll be 70 when I finish with this class, when the funerals are over again and the survivor is proved an Immortal.

I have been an Immortal since I was 34 years old and every mirror I pass tells me I haven't aged a day. I have made the water inside me strong. The essence of my life can now repel death. I was about to start teaching these hundred students how to do the same. One shall pass. The rest will fail. The rest will die.

'I am Lethario Melt, your teacher, and the only thing standing between you and death.'

No class had ever been more attentive.

*

That first class went well, textbook, actually. I wrote the textbook, in fact. So all in all, not that surprising. The pupils listened, jaws dropping but attention never wavering. I was giving them what they wanted, what their families wanted, what we all want. It was on that day I met the one I knew would survive.

Astrid Basque. She wore her robes like a queen but carried herself like a pauper. Her hair was bark brown and her skin candle-wax cream. Her eyes opened and closed like butterfly wings. She might have been a youth of 20, but at that time she was 37, and still she retained those traits. At the end of the lecture she spoke to me: 'Professor Melt, thank you. Thank you so much for this opportunity. I never imagined I'd be the first in my family. What you saw in my application I can't guess. I couldn't even attend the interview. I feared I was too old, that it was too late. You're taking a chance with me. I know it. I won't waste it.'

I was so startled that before I could utter a single syllable she had vanished into the throng. Many in the audience were old enough to have grown-up children and to have started thinking about what the future held. Do not forget that I achieved the great milestone when I was 34, and plenty have done so later in life. My pupils were so grateful for the chance I was giving them but too many arrived in my halls proud and self-assured. Too many made it this far and thought that was far enough. There is no great secret to survival here. Commitment must be absolute. Focus is paramount. That was all it took, yet many lacked these simple traits. Astrid, on the other hand, mixed sincerity with diligence.

I watched Astrid from then on. I may have even shown favouritism, although only when she asked for extra assistance. I would have given the same attention to any pupil that asked it of me but they seldom did. The Immortal

Council and I had selected one hundred from tens of thousands. It was no wonder the victors of this first stage were arrogant.

After almost five years of teaching, only ten of my pupils had died, which was a remarkable count. My techniques were improving class by class. The trials were only two weeks away when Astrid came to me with further gratitude. Pupils were not encouraged to disturb me after the day's lessons had ended; however, it was not forbidden. No one would have denied her passage. I was reading, as was typical, when my guard knocked and announced her. She may have been my pupil and I almost twice her years, but physically our ages were not dissimilar. What followed had been a long time coming, and it was not at first regretted. She left quickly and quietly but at the time I scarcely noticed. During the act I saw something, something in her soul and in her eyes. Something I had never seen before. I did not know how long it had dwelt there.

The next day I was alone again. When I'm not educating I am often thinking, and unlike many I find that thinking is done best when sedentary. There are benches everywhere I am likely to go within the compound. I sat and I thought. I thought about her eyes, but I did not dare imagine them too closely. I've never stared death in the face, nor a serpent, nor a rasp-wraith or a brant, but I wager that if someone could conjure a way to combine them, they would see the night-time eyes of Astrid Basque.

I went to the guard post. They had paper there, and quills and pigeons, for dispatching messages in a hurry. I scrawled a quick note, then tore it up carefully and completely. I rewrote it and, this time satisfied with my handwriting, dispatched it. Vastel, the capital guard, recommended a particular bird when he saw my urgency. It at least made it to the horizon. Only time would tell if it made the journey to Quaste. I retired and cancelled my lessons. Lunch and dinner were brought to my chambers but I could not eat. There is only so much life in the body, so much blood and water. If I were to eat, my heart would direct my blood to my stomach, leaving my mind lacking. I had to think. Even in the best case a note would not return for a week. Had I any other way of confirming my suspicions? No, I hadn't. The library was incomplete when it came to history, lineage, family arms and allegiances. Yet incomplete was better than nothing. I sent for the *Tomes of Riler* and skimmed a thousand random pages before I succumbed to frustration.

A week. One more week would not matter. Nothing I could teach her in that time could make a difference. A threat remained: how much had I already taught her? I had taught her everything.

Seven more of my pupils were dead by the time the pigeon returned. Each one killed by old age in the dead of night, safe in their beds. Nine days had passed since the pigeon had been dispatched and I was at my wits' end. I had refused Astrid every night since then. Every night she had come, every night she had been turned away. Why did she come? That question occupied my mind incessantly. As per my instructions, when the pigeon returned Vastel interrupted my class and cleared the hall of all 83 pupils. I stood before an empty hall and read the note:

'Lethario, I received your letter with great anticipation, quickly overcome by grave concern. Should your suspicions be well-founded I fear for you, and your college. I fear for us all. I rate your judgement of character above that of the Immortal Council but I pray you are wrong. I have traced Astrid Basque's lineage through a thousand years of Quaste history and found Azrael at its head. The girl's family has likely carried the demon throughout the ages, hidden and buried out of sight and mind. Ascertain the truth. If she is his spawn she must be brought to her end.'

So there it was. I was just days away from finishing the resurrection of a thousand year old malevolent deity. In my student days I would probably have given some time to the idea that after a thousand years it might be calmer, perhaps even in a state to benefit from hugs. Today I had my own students to protect and I'd already done a piss-poor job of that. They were nearly all destined to die, but this would render everything they had fought for worthless. They were here in the full knowledge that they risked death but were content to offset that risk against the value of immortality. Take away that chance and it was suddenly better they all live and that none achieve their goals.

The trial was a gruelling affair but it had its place. Azrael, however, was sucking the life out of my students before they were ready and I hadn't noticed until I had seen her eyes. Her whiteless manic eyes. She had sat atop me, stroking my chest gently, as one might touch a delicate, forbidden artwork. She rode me with all the innocence I expected of her. She relished every moment, but sheepishly, only just daring to touch me. It was all in her eyes. But was Astrid Azrael or was Azrael Astrid? Did it even matter?

I had to intervene. Five days remained to me. The first thing to do was follow some scientific principles. I had to replicate the findings of my associate in Quaste. I needed incontrovertible evidence. Whatever Astrid was, I needed to prove she was a danger before I took drastic action against her. I needed assistance. As the capital guard Vastel would have the access I required. I met him, immediately and secretly. He remembered the urgency with which I had sent the letter and agreed to assist, even before I had explained the repercussions of failure.

That night Vastel searched Astrid's dormitory while I decoyed her to my room. During my previous rebuttals I had given the somewhat flimsy excuse of excessive academic labour as we neared the date of the trial. My invitation declared that I was of a mind to rest at last.

My evening thus far had been spent steeling myself for whatever might occur once she was in my chambers. I would refuse her if necessary and we would talk. She arrived promptly; I suppressed a shiver as I let her in. I had thought it a mirage but she was growing ever more beautiful each day.

My preparations were wasted, for in moments she had disrobed. Her fingers nestled in my hair as she pulled my head down to meet her lips. And it struck me. The eyes, that first night, I had seen the eyes so soon, but I had been unable to detach myself from her. I had wanted to ravish her, I had prayed as I kissed her breasts that the night would never end. Now again I could not move except with her body against mine as we stepped in a waltz towards the bed.

My knees folded against it and I fell backwards, my shirt exposed. Astrid drew it from my arms and climbed onto the bed. My need for her was rising unimaginably. Even when I saw the eyes return, the void was so black yet seemed so full of life. The lives of my students. Even as I saw them my hands were rising up her naked back, running over her shoulders, looping round her arms and caressing her breasts. I could not help myself, and I did not care.

When the night was over she gathered her things but this time she lingered. She thanked me. It was perhaps the most profuse thanks I had ever received, even more so than the first she had given me. The kind of thanks you give to someone when they have saved you from death, freed you from eternal slavery, restored sight to you after a lifetime of blindness, and bestowed a child upon you, all in the same act.

Dear God. I couldn't have made a more severe mistake. I had impregnated her, I, an Immortal. Our first night together had ended in failure and she had returned every night after, desperate to conceive as the trial drew nearer. Now she had succeeded a devastating thought crossed my mind. What if Azrael were not Astrid, but the child she now bore?

Someone banged on the door loudly. My first reaction was to shrink back in terror, but why should she return? Someone called out. It was Vastel. I rushed into my dressing gown – it was late, and this would not be suspect. Except he knew Astrid had been here. I stripped again, dressed in a flash, and let him in.

'Professor, you were starting to worry me,' he confided. 'I saw Miss Basque had departed but when you took so long to answer I feared the result of her visit.'

'The encounter has diminished me, Vastel, and that is all I shall say.' I closed the door behind him after ensuring the corridor remained empty. I needed to sit but Vastel was content to stand. 'So tell me – her room. What did you learn in so little time?'

'Darkness, darkness in the walls.'

I sat up. 'Darkness? Was this a sensation you felt?'

Vastel shook his hands. 'No, no. I saw it. The walls and ceiling have gone dark, the paper and paint charred as if by fire. Large circles of black here and there. There was even one on the floor, mostly hidden under the bed. The carpet had gone black as pitch. But I couldn't smell burning, and it still felt like carpet.'

'What about the smell of paint or dye?' I suggested.

'Just perfume,' he shrugged. 'I suppose that's not what you expected but it is a bit strange, isn't it?'

'Exceedingly,' I said. Images of human sacrifice and cannibalism had pervaded my fears. This was stranger than I had expected, but was it proof? Deaths did accelerate as the trial approached: bold and stupid students tested their strength, sapping life from their fellow pupils. If the culprit could be identified they were punished without mercy, always. On any day but the trial it was murder. But so many, with almost a week to go? It was unlikely, and more than that – I had seen her eyes.

This whole time I had been staring at Vastel, following him as he paced in clinking armour. I hadn't thought him old, but without his helmet he was grey and wrinkled, and seemed to be growing more decrepit by the second.

Vastel wheezed suddenly and halted. The helmet under his arm clattered to the floor and he scrambled to pull off his gauntlet. Underneath, his fingernails had grown long and crooked. His skin had turned grey and his fingers were nothing but bone.

He turned to me and groaned. 'What is this?'

He collapsed into a pile of metal and bone and skin.

I think I screamed then, but I might just have heard his dying breath. I was already fleeing for the door, wondering if even an Immortal would succumb to a demon of death. This was beyond nature.

What had I done?

When I opened the door the first thing I saw was the eyes. Astrid was no more dressed than the last time I had seen her. She was scarcely wearing her robes; her left shoulder was bare almost to the breast. This time there was no lust.

Her voice now matched her eyes. 'He entered a sacred place. He polluted the birthplace of my son.'

Not more than ten minutes had passed since she left my chamber, but now she stood outside it near to term. Her hands cupped her swollen belly and stroked it as innocently as any mother.

I snatched her wrist as she turned to go. 'Astrid, stop! What has possessed you?'

As if I didn't already know the answer.

'You have ignited the seed, Immortal. There is no stopping it.'

Then the screams began. This time I knew they were not mine. They belonged to my students, my students who were all around us, asleep in their beds above and below. My chambers were at the very centre of the college; Astrid was beginning her dark work at its heart.

Where the screams were strongest, where they pierced most sharply, darkness was spreading like lichen. The loudest, most desperate cries came from the room beneath our feet. I heard a girl choke in agony and watched as her pain became soot harrowed into the carpet. Between the dry corpse of Vastel and Astrid, half covering this side of the door, was a circle of black. Vastel's life had been pulled through the wall. Azrael's mark was being charred upon every wall and floor.

I smacked her across the side of the head. My knuckles cracked against her skull and I howled in pain and rage. Astrid struck me in return and I was cast back into my chamber, my door splintering from its hinges at the strength of her blow.

I crawled, concussed, for seconds and minutes and longer. Before I could reach the door again I was being hauled to my feet.

'Professor! Are you all right? The students are screaming. What happened to the capital guard?'

'She sucked the life out of him...' I managed. 'We have to stop her. We have to protect the students.'

My rescuers were both guards. One said to the other: 'The capital's dead. That means you're in charge, Sir.'

Several seconds of silence followed. Vastel's successor was not about to take charge, so I had to. The screaming of my pupils hadn't stopped, but at least many were fleeing from the centre of the college.

'Astrid Basque is murdering my pupils! Wake every student, bring them to the trial hall! And for heaven's sake don't go near her!'

Soldiers need direction. As soon as they had purpose they would do their duty, and do it well.

I made for the trial hall. I had to keep my students together, to keep them calm, to lead them against death itself.

It took an age to reach it. A dozen steps from it, the door above me banged open and a student poked his head in. Jeremy Lambeth. Bright, cocky, tall. He would have had a chance if I hadn't accepted Astrid into my class, or my bed. 'Professor, take my hand.'

Strong as well. He heaved me up the last few steps and ushered me into the trial hall. No more than fifty of my students had managed to take refuge. Half a dozen guards were at the other doors, barring them with desks and chairs.

'Are there no others?' I gasped.

Brandy Seiglet answered. Also cocky, but too young, and not as bright as she appeared. Her chances were much slimmer. 'No one else got away! They all just started dying!'

I looked at the remainder of my class. Eyes wide, nightgowns torn, many of them older and leaner than I had last seen them. They had already had brushes with Astrid, brushes with death. I didn't know how much to tell them. It had to be enough to give them strength without letting them surrender to fear. Should I say that their fellow pupil was siphoning away their lives to feed the seed of a millennium-old demon of death in preparation for his resurrection? And that I helped spawn it? Or just tell them that magic has possessed Astrid and that we must battle it together to save our souls? The second option was infinitely better. I would answer for my crimes when this day was done. Had I controlled myself … but there was no time for self-recrimination. Astrid was descending on us even as we stood shivering.

So I told them. I told them we were facing something that we had never seen before, but that together we could overcome it. To their credit, no-one panicked. There was no shortage of shock, but it dawned on me that these men and women were probably all prepared to die. In a week they would have faced the trial anyway, and all but one of them would have died. I didn't know if that made them fearless or reckless. We would soon see.

'Magic is the curse of our world. We will never be rid of it, we will never control it, but I have taught you to repel it. Today you face your trial.'

Familiar words spoken early. What followed was to be very different. In a real trial I fill the hall with my students and watch. I watch them die, collapsing into ignominy as one, stronger, more focused, more committed than all the rest, draws the life from the others. They fortify their own life with dozens more, enough to stave off death. But repelling Azrael would not be enough. We needed something extraordinary, something desperate.

And we would need it soon. I could see darkness gathering on the main doors. Astrid might be only just beyond them, sucking life out of the room. 'Stand together!' I instructed. 'Focus your strength! Resist her!'

I stood between the door and my students. If anyone could stop her taking life it was me. I hadn't had to concentrate to contain my life in decades, but I could feel Azrael's magic tugging at my soul, willing it away from its body.

The darkness on the door had stopped growing. I would never let her take my students.

The door caved in with a crunch and I hit the ground in a spin, striking my head and tasting blood. I could smell sulphur and burning. My students were screaming again, even the older ones.

Azrael was standing over me wearing the torn, bloody remains of Astrid like a second skin stretched too tight. Her crushed skull was wedged against its shoulder, her exposed ribs protruded from its stomach. It had two curved horns to match a crescent moon and arms as long as spears.

My students were dying, falling to their knees one by one, crying through gritted teeth, holding onto their lives with everything they had. Only someone who had passed the trial could possibly resist, someone who was more than just their own life.

Azrael stepped over me. While the room spun I felt for one of the huge splinters from the door and clutched it in my hand. I climbed to my feet and faced the demon's scaled back. I was the only one here who had passed the trial. Eighty one lives dwelt within me. I had beaten all of them, and earned life ever after. It was time to honour their sacrifice. 'Azrael!'

He ignored me.

'Azrael! I banish you!'

Azrael turned, stung by that word. 'There is nothing you can do to banish me, Immortal.'

I took the splinter in two hands and plunged it into my throat. It would never pierce my ribcage. Just because I don't age, doesn't mean I can't die. Eighty souls burst out of me like water from a dam. With only one exception they had spent the last fifty years desperately struggling to be free. When they found that freedom it was explosive.

Azrael was swept away in a tidal wave of lives, buried in light until there was nothing left but the echo of his roar.

My own soul left more slowly than the rest. It gave me the chance to watch my students rise once more. The overflow of life from my body struck them as well, embracing them. One of my lives entered each of them. They may not live forever, but perhaps it's better that way.

Ithaca, NY

Josh Williams

'This is a police line and beyond that is a crime scene.'

The hero must get to the prize but can't because of the obstacles in his way. In overcoming those obstacles the hero changes and grows.

'Sir, you cannot cross this line.'

Bullshit. You can go right around an obstacle, move it the hell out of the way, or even decide the prize wasn't worth that much anyway and go someplace else.

'Sir, our officers are armed.'

And not one part of that would involve me developing my character or growing in any way.

'Officer,' I say, 'it has taken me an awful long time to get here and I don't appreciate your tone.'

When Odysseus returns home after overcoming the Trojans, the Cyclops, the Sirens, the witch, the gods and the sea, what does he do? Has he changed? Is he better for his travels?

'Sir, I don't get paid to deliver instructions in a tone that you might care for. I get paid to make sure that you do not cross this line.'

Sure he's a little older, but as he proceeds to say 'hi' to his dog, kill everyone in his house and take his wife to bed, he's not thinking about the journey.

'Officer?' I say again, drawing out a cigarette, 'do you have a light?'

But this time I did need to get to that prize, whatever it took. I missed my dog.

*

I'd been away too long. Ithaca was Ithaca, but the place I used to live was now a crime scene, and she wasn't there anymore. I'd have to track her down.

'Hello, Mrs Travers.' I used my best telephone manner.

'I know that voice.'

'Sure you do, Mrs...'

The phone went dead. She'd recognised me just fine.

'...Travers. I'm looking for your daughter.'

I tried the other number. He answered and this time I put on someone else's voice altogether.

'Good afternoon, this is Big Rock 97.3 FM and we're trying to locate a … er … a Penny Travers so she can claim the monthly prize.'

I could hear the breathing at the other end but couldn't tell if he'd bought that or seen right through it.

'Prize money,' I added.

'Well, okay, yeah. You can reach Penny at this number if you need to,' and he reeled off the ten digits. 'And how much are we talking, you know, for the...'

This time I hung up.

*

'Hey.' After all that, I didn't have much to say.

'Who's ... is that you?'

She dropped to a whisper.

'It's me.'

'You can't come around here, Jimmy, you know what they'll do. And where the hell have you been all this time?'

'It's been a while. But I'm here now.'

'No you're not!' Her voice rose. 'They'll know you the moment you show up, and who says you're wanted here anyway, Jimmy? Who says?'

'Just tell me where you are, Penny, so I can see you. We can talk, and if you want, then I can go.' I waited, but she was quiet. 'You still have Lady?'

'She's fine.'

I waited some more.

'We're on 3rd, 3rd and Grant.'

'Pen, I...' but for the second time today the phone just hummed, disconnected.

*

Penny had taken a room in a shared house. Shared with the same old gang we used to run with, same old gang as would be only too pleased to see me. But there's a way to clear a house full of people who would kill you if they saw you – tell them you're somewhere else. And when they've all gone there, find out what the hell Penny is doing, living with these weasels.

'You weren't here so you don't get to judge.'

'Yeah, but...' I was starting to whine.

'Yeah, but, what? How long do you think before they realise you aren't in our old house? You think the police outside it won't put them off?'

'Ah, shit, I only owe them a bit of money.'

'And I told them I wouldn't look at another man until you were dead.'

'Ah. Shit.'

'We are still married. Aren't we?' She glared at me.

'Yeah, sure, honey. Sure we are. And I came to say, you know, would you come with me?'

'Come where, Jimmy, where have you been?'

'You know what happens when I get near money, Pen, it calls to me.'

'And?'

'And sometimes I can't resist, you know...'

'And?' She folded her arms and started to tap her foot on the hardwood flooring.

'I got waylaid for a while,' I paused, 'at the State's pleasure. Got caught by a security camera. Me and a bunch of others, but...' I swallowed the taste of confinement out of my mouth and looked about. 'Lady?'

I whistled.

A dog's claws scratched at the back porch and Penny opened the door to a crazy-looking hound, big and brown and teeth and ears. 'Lady!' The dog scrabbled over me, licking my face and almost knocking me to the floor. 'Whoa there! Down, dog.'

Penny smiled for the first time since I'd seen her. 'She won't let anyone else go near her.'

I grabbed at Lady's collar and spun it round to see the name tag.

'And no one does that,' she said.

'It just says "Lady", on this little disc shaped like a key.' I replied, smiling too.

'Key?' Penny shook her head.

'Key.' I said, and looked from one to the other. 'You two ladies want to come with me? Via a deposit box, obviously, but then, I don't know, someplace far from here?'

Lady barked and Penny casually shushed her like she always did.

*

The hero needs to get to the prize, but can't because of all those nasty barriers in his way. In order to overcome, he must change and grow. But sometimes, sometimes you just come over to get the key to the obstacle before leaving with the real prize, and heading, well, heading who cares where?

Cherry Popper

Alana James

Cherry lay down on her back on the bed and sighed. The room depressed her. These four walls had been the same since she was fourteen: smeared with a sickly pink design her cash-strapped mum picked out. Three years later the paper was peeling and stained yellow from her fags. Cherry half turned over to rummage in the drawer of her bedside table. A handful of empty neon wrappers fell to the floor before she found an unused johnny.

'Here, you know what to do with it don't you?' She tossed it to the kid in the baseball cap hunched at the foot of the bed. He snorted and tried to look cool, but Cherry had seen it all before. No matter how hard they were around the estate, when she had them in here they fumbled like little boys. Least he didn't try and talk to her like some of them did. She wriggled to the bottom of the bed, pulled down her knickers 'til they were hanging off one ankle, then lay back down with her mini skirt yanked up, legs open. It made her feel like she was at the fucking doctors, waiting. *Why am I always waiting for something?* Cherry wondered dismally. Waiting for her mum to kick out the latest alcho she called a boyfriend, waiting for the smell of sick to leave the living room, waiting for life to get better than this.

'Fuck's sake, Chris, get a move on will you.' From somewhere between her legs she heard the rustle of his trackie pants round his knees, but still nothing. Cherry dragged her head up. He was staring at her like he'd never seen a woman before, which she knew he hadn't in real life.

Eventually she felt the poke of his sweaty fingers on her thighs, then with a shuffle and a grunt he went in. It hurt, always did, but Cherry's mind disconnected from that part of herself.

Chris was nothing special, just the latest recruit to the gang that ran this part of the estate. He dressed the same as the others, carried his flicker in his sock and talked crap. Cherry hung around them when she was bored or needed to get high. *I'll get by without tonight,* she promised herself. She couldn't face all that macho crap. Johnno had been going on and on about the tagging they were gonna do along the East London train line, like it'd prove something. *That gang of idiots never proved nothin' to me, nothing worth proving anyway.* Sometimes Cherry regretted that she'd never been one to make friends with girls. Mothers warned their daughters not to get too close to her. They weren't frightened she'd lead them astray, everyone round here was stray, but Cherry might sleep with their fathers. It didn't worry her; while women could make your life hell, men were the key to surviving.

The banging down below her skirt had got going; a steady thud, thud, thud that made her hips jig up and down. The top half of her body was motionless, her eyes half shut. She thought about lighting a fag but the effort overwhelmed her.

Through the thin flat walls a door slammed open then shut. Cherry heard her mother ricochet off the walls. *Drunk again*, Cherry knew without even seeing her slack face.

'You there, love?' her mum slurred out and a man's voice laughed, saying something Cherry didn't want to hear. From the sound of things her mum and the guy who might be her boyfriend were trying to stagger their way down the hall.

Cherry looked down at Chris. The stupid twat was frozen in place, mouth gawping open. She swore she felt him slowly shrivel up.

'You said we'd have the place to ourselves!' he hissed at her. *Shit, this was going to take forever now.*

'Fuck off, Mum, I'm busy!' she shouted. That's all it ever took, a shout and they were gone. The responding thud told her that her mother and her lover had made it to the other bedroom. 'It's fine, Chris, get a move on.'

Business below her waist hesitantly resumed. It wasn't guys like Chris you had to be afraid of, Cherry reckoned. It was the ones in charge: the bigger ones, the ones with the connections, the psychos that made her blood run cold. Rudy got himself killed last year. Hesitated when it mattered. Cherry missed her brother sometimes but he'd always been a liability, everyone knew that.

Instead the only family she had was her mum, who they could hear moaning incoherently. The only thing Cherry felt for her was pity. Unlike her, Cherry got by all right. She was smart, see. She knew all she had in this life was herself, and she handled her assets real well. When puberty hit hard and fast her body expanded in all the wrong places: tits and arse. When she walked suddenly everything bounced, demanding attention. *You wanna watch yourself with those tits, love,* her mum had told her. Eventually Cherry decided fuck it, and dyed her hair deep red, painted her lips to match and walked like she owned her curves and the whole fucking estate to boot.

Cherry thought back to that time and wondered, *If I had left well alone, would anything have turned out different?*

She rolled her head slowly over to the side so she could see the man-boy still trying to give it to her, baseball cap jerking up and down. He was holding her knees with the cups of his palms now, though she hadn't felt him do it. It looked like he was trying to hold himself steady, like it was all too much for him really. His face grimaced with the twin exertions of pleasure and intense concentration. They all thought they should hold on, not let out too soon. Like Cherry gave a shit.

No, she thought, things would have turned out worse. Finally the guys would have taken what they wanted. This way she got something out of it too. That's how come she got her nickname, Cherry Popper. All the new gang members had to sleep with her if they wanted respect. In exchange the gang didn't take without permission and looked out for her, stopped anyone else messing with her. Sex was a raw deal but it bought Cherry her freedom.

Bored now, she shoved one hand under the waistband of her skirt, fingers expertly groping. She let herself start to feel something, her hand beginning to work out some of the knots in her head. *Better, better...* It was hard to concentrate though with the kid still at her. She decided to put them both out of their misery and began to pump her hips against his. Chris lifted his head in surprise, a high-pitched gasp escaping his throat before he could stop it. He thrust into her once more, only reaching halfway before shooting his load.

Cherry made sure he withdrew with the johnny still on, watched him tie it like a balloon and shove it in his pocket for proof, pull up his pants and leave. With the room around her completely still now, she worked her fingers back down and reclaimed her body.

'Cherry Popper' was awarded second prize in the National Association of Writers' Groups 2012 Short Story with a Given Phrase competition.

Indian Summer

Steve Partridge

I arrived at my mother's house at three, on the afternoon of Monday the 21st August, still jet-lagged from the flight home from New York. The first time I had visited her for nearly three months. The scent of an apple wood fire, from the house across the road, drifted on the breeze into her garden. We sat in the conservatory as she fussed and fiddled, laying a hand embroidered linen table cloth on a glass top table. A cloth she had stitched herself, after she had become engaged to my father in 1933.

She looked up and said: 'The boys have gone down to the green to watch the cricket. When the cricketers go in for tea at four o'clock they'll come back here to join us. I've made scones and a fruitcake, and we've got some homemade raspberry jam with clotted cream. Just like we used to have when you were a boy.'

She smiled at me and laughed a little.

'Do you remember the first time we had scones with jam and cream? You got stung by a wasp. Oh, you did make a noise.'

'I think I was only two, Mum, so I don't actually remember, but you have told me that story before.'

In the centre of the table there was a Royal Albert cake stand. On the top plate, there were freshly baked scones with sultanas. On the bottom plate, slices of homemade fruitcake with cherries. Next to the cake stood two porcelain dishes, one contained raspberry jam, the other one filled with clotted cream. A silver spoon pushed into the contents of each dish.

'I put a drop of dark rum in the fruit cake, your dad likes that.'

She handed me a small pile of five plates which matched the decoration on the cake stand.

'Put the plates round, Dave – save me stretching over with my creaky old hips.'

I started to place the plates around the table, then looked at my mother and said:

'Mum … who is coming to tea?'

She looked at me and giggled, like I'd asked a stupid question.

'Guess?'

'Well, Dad I suppose?'

My voice trailed off a little, as I said it.

'Yes. And who else? Who does he always go to cricket with?'

'I don't know, Mum. Who does he go to cricket with?'

'Doug and Pete of course! They always go to cricket together.'

I looked into her blue-grey eyes, and saw her as I did when I was a child. My mum: warm, loving, funny and tender. The centre of my world.

My uncles, Douglas and Peter, both passed away in the early 1990s. And my father died in August 2000. When my father was courting my mother in the thirties he watched cricket with her brothers many times. Mostly the village team, but there had also been excursions on the train to Southampton to watch Hampshire and every now and again, a trip to London to see a test match. When I was a child, in the fifties, I was brought up on stories of Len Hutton and Maurice Leyland beating the Australians at the Oval in 1938.

I said, 'Oh yes, Mum, daft of me to forget. Not much of a day for it though is it?'

'A bit overcast, but that's alright at this time of the year. You know what that means, Dave, don't you?'

We chorused the answer together and laughed out loud.

'We are going to have an Indian summer!'

'You always say that, Mum. But it doesn't necessarily happen.'

'Oh look, it's four o'clock, they'll be home soon. I'll pour the tea.'

My mother poured the milk into the cups first, as she had always done, then the tea. She laughed her little laugh. And mouthed some words silently to herself as she concentrated on pouring the tea, careful not to let any drip from the spout of the teapot into the saucers.

'Happens most of the time,' she said. 'It won't be long before those Red Indians are here, riding their ponies up and down the road.'

We both laughed out loud again. When I was younger we had argued about the origins of Indian summers. I had always said they came from India, and the expression had been added to the English language by civil servants returning home after a tour of duty with The British Raj. She had always insisted, on good authority from my grandmother, Indian summers had originated in North America. She said the early settlers in North America feared late bursts of sustained sunshine in the autumn, because they knew they would be at risk from attack by Indians. But, if the snow came fast at the end of the fall, they wouldn't have to worry about the Indians again until the following spring. We left the argument there. Neither of us bothering to do any research to find out the truth of the matter. Both of us happy to beg to differ.

When it got to five o'clock, she said: 'Look at all this cold tea. What are those boys up to? I bet they've gone to the clubhouse for a pint. They've done that before! And I told them you were coming today!'

As we started to clear the table of the tea things, my mind drifted back to when I was child and what she told me about Indian summers. They were a kind of metaphor to her, a necessary optimistic view of the future. We both knew we had to have a winter, but just before it started to get cold, there would, in her mind at least, always be the chance of a final burst of sunshine and warmth. An Indian summer before an early frost bit hard into the ground and finished off the late flowering shrubs.

When I was a child, agitated and tearful, she said, as she tucked me in: 'Go to sleep, Dave, it will be all right in the morning.'

And it always was. A shaft of sunlight through the curtains, milky porridge with a sugary crust, Marmite on toast, the dull slap of the letter box flap when my comic was delivered. A smile and a chuckle across the breakfast table.

Her Indian summers felt like those, "it will be alright in the morning" things, comforting, something beautiful to dream about, a translucent autumnal patina at the end of a disappointing summer. Turner's soft, hazy, impressionist light, gentle warmth in the breeze like the body heat of a sleeping cat, crimson leaves on a Japanese cherry tree. Cameo clips from cerebral home movies recorded in my memory, and then played, and replayed, like a favourite film, during quiet moments of reflection.

I hugged her, and said I wouldn't leave it so long before I visited her again. Knowing, only too well, it was a promise I probably wouldn't keep. As I left, she looked at me, smiled and said: 'Just remember, Dave, we will have an Indian Summer this year. You wait and see.'

In mid-October of 2002 my mother had a stroke and passed away peacefully at home. She was 90 years old. She'd had a good life and lived it well. It was only in the last four or five years her memory started playing tricks on her, when she saw, heard, and believed things that weren't real. For the greater part of her life she was sharp and alert, fully *compos mentis.*

*

It's late October. My mother's funeral cortège is moving silently forward in soft buttermilk sunshine. A man in a morning coat with a black silver-tipped cane and a top hat walks in front of a creeping hearse. Three polished cars follow with a brother and sister, in-laws, children, grandchildren, nieces and nephews. Friends walk close behind, some with sticks and light winter coats, others with small talk and tears. A warm breeze quietly waves across the crematorium grounds.

An avenue of maple trees bright with red and orange leaves stand to attention in her honour, like colour sergeants on parade. From behind them, I think, I see, a quick flash of feathered bonnets and hear the muffled sound of horses' hooves. We stop at the chapel of rest. Her coffin slides gently forward. The pallbearers drop their shoulders underneath, one, two, three, lift and move. The priest looks on, benign and proper, a cross on his chest and reverence in his eyes. The holy bible enshrined in his hands, his contradictions, folded neatly into the pages of his soul.

Without warning, from behind the maples the Arapahos appear, the sound of hooves rumbling like thunder now, twenty or more on their snorting piebald ponies. A shaman at their head, they whoop and shout, fierce painted faces, eagle-feathered war bonnets, buckskins, bows and spears. Taking her from the bearers they lay her on a travois. A drum beats, and the braves dance and chant in elegiac celebration until the maples have shed their leaves. We stand, as still as herons in a stream, watching and waiting.

On the breeze I catch the slightest whiff of fruitcake and dark rum, the clink of a spoon on a porcelain cup, the acidic smoothness of raspberry jam and clotted cream on the top of my tongue. Turning, the Arapahos trot away on noiseless hooves through the air, gliding my mother over the garden of remembrance and across the fields. We all look up in silence. The priest crosses himself and the shaman glances back. Then, in a moment, she is gone … away home, to Wyoming.

In Full Flow

Judy Hodgetts

I sit in a cramped wooden boat as it inches its way through water that is dark and sludgy. My throat burns with the stench of stagnation. Overhanging trees, dense and unwelcoming, frame the narrow strip of river. Whatever lies below the surface is hidden and I have no interest in dipping my fingers into something unknown. I use what energy I have to look around for oars, but there are none. I shrug, accepting that's the way it is.

You could end this misery at any time. A bottle of pills taunts me as it rolls around at my feet. But my mind is fuzzy and I am unable to focus. I close my eyes and allow the boat to lead me somewhere unplanned, unknown.

Weeks, maybe months, pass until the boat shudders to a halt, stopped in its journey by a dam. I stare at layer upon layer of debris – twigs and branches twisted together, small pebbles packed among huge boulders, slimy with moss. I don't know what to do. Acid bubbles up in my stomach and into my throat. My chest tightens with the familiar feeling of panic. There is movement in the water and I bury my head in my hands, too frightened to look. A long time passes as I listen to unfamiliar noises, and then I peep through my fingers to see the blockage being removed piece by piece.

'We didn't build the dam,' the strangers tell me as they swim away. 'It was all down to you.'

A small amount of tension has lifted from my shoulders and it feels easier to breathe. I lean back to find I have a cushion behind me. I feel lighter, but I still don't know where

I'm going. The river opens out slightly, the bushes either side now allowing small chinks of light through. The water is less dark, but still murky, and reveals nothing of what lies below. Pieces of rubbish float on it, around the boat. As I stare at them, uncomfortable and long-buried memories rise to the surface of my mind. I shudder and lean out of the boat, trying to push the junk away, and it moves just out of reach.

My boat continues to drift, but when I wake, the sun is glistening on the water. Turquoise water that reflects the rays back at me. The banks either side have opened up as if in welcome, showing off multi-coloured flowers that sway in the breeze. I smile as I breathe in their aromatic scent. The boat glides through the water before stopping, blocked by another, smaller dam. I ask for help, saying the words out loud. It is less difficult than I think and I laugh as friends swim towards me.

'Come and join us,' they call out as they carefully remove the debris. I jump into the cool water and the sense of freedom, of liberation, is exhilarating.

I climb back on board, surprised to see a seat at the front of the craft now. I sit in it and start the engine. There is a fork in the river ahead of me, and habitual doubts of indecision rush in to mock me. But voices in my head remind me I am capable of deciding where to go. I take a deep breath and steer the boat to the left. It is my boat, my call. At the next dam I stop the boat, reaching out to hurl the stones away to clear my path. These heavy weights are no longer needed and I will not let them affect my life. My hands hurt and my fingers bleed, but I am breathless with the adrenaline rush. I restart the engine with confidence, with a purpose.

I cruise along river after river, happy with the choices I'm making. I find myself in a bay in the Mediterranean and I stretch out in the sunshine, feeling relaxed. Behind me, dramatic mountains rise up, shielding me, keeping me safe. In front, the open sea is vast and limitless, exciting, inviting. I put my anchor down, choosing to stay in the comfort of the bay for now. The boat rocks me to sleep in the swell of the ocean, rhythmical, soothing.

I sit at the front of my boat, filling my lungs with fresh air before setting off. The journey, the adventure, is mine and I am completely in control. I can sail my boat to wherever I like. I can invite friends or I can be alone. These are my decisions to make. I start the engine and my boat moves forward, slicing through water that churns with excitement and opportunities. I laugh as it rides the waves, the salty spray showering me, tangy on my lips. I have no map and yet I don't feel frightened – I know where I'm heading.

SELECT BIOGRAPHIES

Robert Billing

Robert Billing writes hard science fiction and non-fiction, mainly about computers. Educated in Cambridge in the 1970s he has worked in industries as diverse as finance and petrochemicals. He now freelances as a consulting software engineer. He has had two books published, and a number of short stories and technical articles.

Claire Dyer

Claire Dyer's poetry has been published in magazines and anthologies and her first collection, *Eleven Rooms*, is published by Two Rivers Press. Her novels, *The Moment* and *The Perfect Affair*, and her short story, *Falling for Gatsby* are published by Quercus.

Claire is currently undertaking an MA in Poetry at Royal Holloway, University of London. Visit her website at *www.clairedyer.com*.

Judy Hodgetts (aka Judy Bryan)

Judy Hodgetts has self-published three women's fiction novels: *Playground Politics, Beyond the Clouds* and *Behind Closed Doors*. She is now concentrating on writing for children. Having previously worked with disabled children, she has written many stories for them over the years. These children have been her inspiration, her passion – and some of her harshest critics!

Alana James

Alana James has been a member of Reading Writers since 2007 and was the editor of the previous anthology, *Another Light Raid*, which was released in 2011. Her short stories have been published in anthologies and magazines, in print and online.

Hanne Larsson

Hanne Larsson is a bilingual Swede whose mother taught her that every stone is a troll in hiding. She writes, bakes and plays board games, but not necessarily in that order.

Steve Partridge

Steve Partridge writes short fiction and short non-fiction. He also enjoys reading, Chicago blues, theatre, classical concerts, comedians, banter and football.

Julie Roberts

Dashing Regency heroes and damsels in distress have fanned the flames of romance and daring in Julie's novels. Winner of several short story competitions, her themes range from the perfect robotic man to phobic ants, interwoven with six published poetry anthologies. Energy-driven Julie is a speaker to social groups and donates her fees to her local Air Ambulance. Visit *www.jeevestories.co.uk*.

John Shepherd

John Shepherd has written all his life, his first pieces being published while he was still at school. However, he was thirty before he got paid for anything he had written. His earnings from writing have remained embarrassingly small. John won the poetry prize at the 2005 Poole Literary Festival. He loves travelling and his entries here are accounts of trips made in 2005 to Africa and 2013 to Costa Rica.

Eve Wibberley (aka Jennifer Smith)

Eve has been scribbling for years – from fairytales as a child to letters from abroad while living in the Sudan and Sierra Leone. She successfully campaigned for the recognition of dyslexia as a special educational need, writing numerous articles, letters and pamphlets. As a partner in Jeeve Publishing, Eve has contributed to the writing and publishing of several collections including *Fish Pie and Laughter*, *The Guilty Suitcase* and *The Virgin Sardine*. Visit *www.jeevestories.co.uk*.

Charles Whittaker

Charles Whittaker has been a member of Reading Writers for six years. Mainly, he writes short stories and poetry. In 2012 he published a 150-page local history, *Sacred Heart Parish, Henley-on-Thames: A Pugin Legacy*. He holds degrees in Economics, Humanities and English (Masters) and has a Diploma in Creative Writing.

Tahereh Zoghi Javady

Tahereh Zoghi Javady writes short stories, poems and autobiographical work, blending a philosophical Persian outlook with a modern twist. She has a BA Honours in English Literature and European Cultural History, and has also completed a course in Creative Writing. A member of Reading Writers since 1987, her poem 'Time' appeared in their 2005 anthology, and two more – 'The Scar' and 'The Sky Dark or Blue' – in the 2011 anthology. Her first personal collection of poems, *Storms of the Heart*, was published in 2013. Find out more about her writing and current projects at *www.taherehzoghi.com.*

ANOTHER LIGHT RAID

Reading Writers' 2011 anthology, ANOTHER LIGHT RAID, contains poetry, fiction and nonfiction by sixteen local authors and is available both as a print book and an eBook.

'This anthology contains some of the best writing going on in Reading...' says award-winning local thriller writer Patrick Lennon in his introduction.